GRASS WITHOUT LIMITS

Personal Freedom, Family, Faith & ForeverLawn

PRAISE

Book Endorsements

I have to admit, I didn't know what to expect when Dale Karmie gave me this book and told me to give him my honest opinion. Well, not only did I enjoy reading *Grass Without Limits*, but it absolutely reinforced my belief in what it takes to ultimately succeed in business and in life! Dale and Brian would call this unwavering conviction to succeed "the Karmie way," I call it—two brothers who tag teamed their American Dream to the ground and submitted it!!

Jason Cameron
Licensed Contractor & Host of DIY Network's Sledgehammer, Desperate Landscapes & Man Caves

A very good read. A true life story about two families on a make or break journey that is both captivating and inspiring. It is not just about business. It is a life message from The One who orchestrates ordinary events to carry us through life's extraordinary challenges, even those that appear self—inflicted. All to show us a love without limits. An amazing testimony and a remarkable journey. This is a business that is fun to be close to.

Davis Lee
Founding Partner, InnovaNet

To say Dale and Brian Karmie have determination, resolve, and character would be an understatement. During my association with them, it has been a rewarding experience for me to watch these fine men travel the ups and downs of their journey in business and with their family relationships. I have watched them face adversity and never waiver in their principles or their faith in God. I would like to thank them for the relationship that we have built together both professionally and personally. They have been an inspiration for me, my family, and my business. This world could use more genuine character like the Karmie's demonstrate every day in their lives.

Tom Peeples
President, Universal Textile Technologies

Grass Without Limits is an intimate look at the journey of two men who "practice what they preach." Through their ups and downs they stayed settled that no matter what happened things would work out. Having seen first hand many of their "trials," I can say that I was personally challenged and encouraged to see their reliance on faith and family to anchor them. The Karmie's story will make you laugh, cry and encourage you in your journey to your God given destiny.

David A. Standridge
Business Owner, Attorney, and
Author of *Reclaiming the Warrior Spirit*

Grass Without Limits is a masterpiece. It has all the markings of a great novel suspense, comedy, tragedy, exhilaration, and triumph. It also teaches timeless principles which will inspire people towards personal growth and achievement. For anyone looking to do more with their life, *Grass Without Limits* will serve as a true confirmation that the impossible is possible.

Michael B. Ross
Professional Speaker, Author, Coach, and Podcaster
Author of *Building You* and *Overcoming the Character Deficit*

TABLE OF CONTENTS

Preface
Acknowledgments

Conclusion

PREFACE

The idea of writing this book has been on our minds for years. We wanted to share our experiences so that it may help or encourage others. Whether it is entrepreneurs, business professionals, workers, stay-at-home parents, students, or anyone else, there are truths we learned in our journey that are timeless and true that could strengthen you.

We recorded our thoughts independently—no collaboration. Not until the editors started to blend the stories into one did we sit down and review it to make sure it all tied together. Our recollection of the events was amazingly the same. We only say "amazingly" because we are dealing with details that are a decade removed. We hope that our story will entertain you.

Ultimately though, the purpose of this book is to share the truth of who God is and what He has done in our lives through Christ. It is our hope that our trials and perseverance can somehow affect people for the good; that this artificial turf business we have been blessed with can be used to impact those around us—both directly by the products we provide and the business opportunities that ForeverLawn creates. We hold the hope that our story and our experiences can somehow impact others in a more meaning-ful, eternal way.

Life is a story, and stories are meant to be shared. This writing process has been an enjoyable but humbling experience. It's exciting to look back and remember the ride, but humbling to realize how many others have helped us along the way.

There is vulnerability in sharing such a personal story. Our biggest fear in writing this is that it comes off as a boast of our experiences. We have been impacted by so many people's stories. Our greatest hope is that God can use our story to encourage others the way we've been encouraged. As you read this, we pray you won't just see our story but you'll see your own. We started our journey together, but we share this story through each of our voices, allowing you to take this personal adventure with both of us. We pray you'll be encouraged to live your life abundantly and then be willing to share it with others.

ACKNOWLEDGMENTS

Dale

As I reviewed our "story," it was amazing to me how much information we can't include—how many stories weren't recounted and how many names not mentioned. I can't cover them all, and won't even try, but I'd like to add a few acknowledgments to this book.

I would like to thank my wife, Lorie. You are my helpmate and my encourager. You have always loved, trusted, and always believed. We've faced many challenges, but you've never wavered. I love you! My kids; Derek, Kaylyn, Makenna, JenniLee, Colton, are my joy and the reason I press on. You make life fun. I continue striving to be the man you think I am. Thank you for your unconditional love. Brian, I want to thank you for being the better part of our dynamic duo, and for sending that email. Thank you to Angie, Julia, Paige, Meredith, and Ava for allowing your husband/father to chase his dreams, and for being his biggest cheerleaders. Mom, you are an incredible woman. You raised us well. Thank you for all the sacrifices you made. You are a legacy maker. Dad, you were simply the most dedicated, hardest working, driven individual I have ever known. You are gone, but your impact lives forever. Thank you to my in-laws, Jerry, Janet, Donna, and Bryan, for receiving me into your family, and for all the time and love you have poured into me and my family. Thank you to my brothers, Jim and Ken, because you sharpen my axe whenever I am with you. I couldn't have picked any better.

Thank you to my extended family. God has placed me in the center of the finest family (both sides) I could ever ask for. Thank you to my ForeverLawn family for buying into our vision and turning dreams into realities. To the group of brave entrepreneurs and risk takers, the ForeverLawn Dealers, I pray your success will far surpass what we have started. Shelby, Tom, and Bryan Peeples—your belief in us when ForeverLawn was just starting is amazing. I thank God for bringing you into our lives. Thank you to Michael Ross. You are a man of integrity and character. You have impacted my life. David Standridge, because you went through the fires with us, and always encouraged us, thank you. To all the inspirational leaders and prayer warriors, so many people in our business and personal lives have invested time and effort encouraging us and lifting us up in prayer. If you are reading this, you know who you are. Thank you.

Brian

I have been truly blessed and I am very thankful for all the abundant things in my life. There are too many people for me to try and list them all by name, but there are some who deserve great credit. I am thankful to my Lord and Savior Jesus Christ. Without His grace, mercy, and providence, I am just a lost soul. I am thankful for Angie, my wife and best friend, without whom I'd never have the courage or belief to have even attempted this business. I am thankful for my beautiful girls Julia, Paige, Meredith, and Ava, who are worth more to me than they will ever know. I am thankful for my Mom, Dad, Jim, Ken, and Ty, who have shaped who I am. I am thankful for the Linger family whose support and love has been more than I ever imagined. I am thankful for our ForeverLawn team. Without them, ForeverLawn could never have grown into a multi-million dollar international business. I want to thank our ForeverLawn Dealers who truly are the heartbeat of Forever-Lawn. When the opportunity roars, chase your lions because great things are ahead. I am thankful for all of those listed and so many more who have touched my life and helped to make me, and this business, what we are today.

CHAPTER ONE

The Tale of Two Brothers

Dale

It had been a beautiful fall Ohio day in 2002. I gripped the gear shifter in the Ford F-350, hoping to muster the courage to shift from park to drive. Behind me were my home, wife, and kids; ahead of me was the road. I longed to get out of the truck and walk back into the house. Yet, at the same time, I knew our future was calling me to travel the narrow road.

It was after midnight and the house was dark. A few neighborhood lights glimmered as Lorie stood in the driveway staring at me while waiting to see me off. Her eyes looked sad, yet she feigned a smile and gentle wave. Knowing that Brian was waiting for me to pick him up, I forced myself to shift into drive and ease out of my driveway.

As I pulled onto the street, I cast a final glance over my shoulder. I realized things would never be the same. I had no idea how they would change, or how much they would change, I knew only that they would. Questions raced through my mind. How would we ever get the house ready to sell? Would the house even sell once we got it ready? What would we do if it didn't? I had recently taken out a home equity loan and was using that money to fund, in part, this journey we were about to begin. That loan would now be a burden as we tried to sell the house.

I looked in the rear view mirror and saw the trailer that had consumed most of the day to prepare and pack. After getting home from church, I had spent the day putting the side rails on the trailer. I had filled the trailer as much as I could with the items that I thought we would need.

My motorcycle was back there along with a sofa, a couple of suitcases, hand tools, shovels, rakes, and hand tampers. I wondered what I had forgotten. I wish I could have spent the day just holding the kids and talking with Lorie. Instead, I was working and packing frantically trying to get ready for the trip. My son, Derek (age 9), and daughter, Kaylyn (age 7), had been hanging around trying to help. They offered to carry things to the truck and do whatever else needed to be done. I don't think they really understood what was going on, but they knew I needed help.

My younger daughter, Makenna, just wanted me to hold her. She was only four. That's what four year olds do. I would take a break here and there to hold her, but so many things still needed to be finished. As much as I loved the attention from the kids, I had to focus on the job at hand. I had to get ready to leave. How ironic that I couldn't spend time with them because I was preparing to go away from them—for who knows how long.

It was a little over an hour to Brian's house. That was plenty of time to struggle with all the thoughts and questions racing around my head. Could we make it in Albuquerque? Would this crazy idea work? I was on the verge of quitting my lucrative career as a software consultant to move across the country and begin selling artificial turf. Had I really thought this through? Was Brian as scared as I was? Had I not known Brian was waiting for me, I doubt I would have ever pulled out of my driveway. However, he was waiting, and so I pressed on.

Brian

There I was, waiting on Dale. It was after midnight. Where was he? My daughters, Julia and Paige, were sound asleep. Angie and I sat in our living room in our small ranch house without much left to say. We didn't want Dale to watch us fight through tearful goodbyes so we took care of that earlier. I was ready to hit the road. I wasn't sure I had the strength to do it—to leave my wife and two daughters, drive 25 hours across the country to start a business I knew nearly nothing about, in a place where I knew no one. The one thing I was sure of; Dale was coming and I couldn't let him down.

We had talked and prayed about it. We knew this was right. It was crazy for sure, but it was right. If we were in it together, we'd make it, we always had. We also always had fun doing it. But why hadn't he shown up yet? Was there a problem with the truck or trailer? The Ford F-350, which we nicknamed "Big Blue," seemed like a solid vehicle, but it was a used truck. It was our first purchase related to this new business venture. Rather than let my head run wild, I picked up the phone and called Dale. He was still an hour away in his driveway tying down the load on the trailer. My heart sank, more waiting. I'm sure I spent the time holding and comforting Angie, but I really don't remember much more than staring down my driveway waiting for those headlights. Finally, the headlights came—about three hours late but they came. Together, Dale and I began our journey 2,000 miles across the country. There would be many more times like this. Times when I didn't know if I could go on, whether it was worth it, whether I was good enough. Honestly, I quit several times, and Dale quit several as well: fortunately, we just never quit on the same day. More importantly, we never quit on each other or our families.

Brian

CHAPTER TWO

The Backstory

Dale

Great journeys seem like they should have a lot of fanfare. Does this mean this journey wouldn't be great? It was after 4:00 a.m. Angie was the only person there waving goodbye. I was tired; probably more tired than a person should be at the start of a 30-hour cross-country trip. This was how our journey began. Not a lot was said between us as we started out. I am guessing this had every bit as much to do with how scared we were as how tired we were.

As we rolled down the highway, I began reflecting on what had brought us to this point. Brian and I had first started discussing the idea of selling artificial grass about seven months prior in February of 2002. I had forwarded an online article about Mount Union College making the decision to install a turf field. I had simply sent it on as a point of interest. However, Brian read the article and then followed some of the links at the bottom of the page. In the end, he stumbled across the AstroLawn website. AstroLawn was a company that sold artificial turf for landscapes and homes. Intrigued, he sent me this seemingly innocuous note, "Hey, check this out. This would be killer in the Desert Southwest."

As I have heard many times in the past, words mean things. Those twelve words were the start of a journey I could not have imagined. Something about that comment, that thought, stuck in my head. A week or two later, Brian was at my house and I questioned him on his email. He seemed a little surprised, and in some manner told me that he had not thought much more about it. We jokingly commented that we should call the company and find out what it was all about. A few minutes later, we were on the phone with AstroLawn.

The Backstory

There is something about a crazy idea that gets me going. It did then, and it still does today. Artificial grass for your home definitely qualified as a crazy idea. While it seemed legitimate enough to be a real opportunity, it was also wild enough to scare and thrill us at the same time. Could we do something like this? Would anyone buy it? Was there a chance something like this would ever catch on? What could happen if it did?

Brian

It was just a simple email, nothing more, nothing less. I didn't give it much forethought, and I didn't have grandiose plans. It was just an email and it was harmless as far as I was concerned. I had just finished reading about a local college putting in a synthetic turf field. Dale and I both worked from our homes as consultants for a boutique software consulting firm. We shot back and forth simple emails all the time. However, this one would be different. This one would change the course of our lives.

I was never really a fan of artificial turf fields. Hearing of our favorite local college putting in a "fake" field caught me off guard. Football was meant to be played in the grass, dirt, and mud. We are in Northeast Ohio—the birthplace of football. Why play such a pure sport on a fake field? I decided to follow some links from the article on the stadium project to learn a little more about this new generation of artificial turf fields. It wasn't carpet like, it had individual grass blades that were a couple inches tall and even had a rubber or sand substance taking the place of soil. Chasing one link to another to learn about this weird new product, something caught my eye. People were putting this stuff in their yards? That seemed odd, but I was intrigued.

Having been born and raised in the Midwest, something else had grabbed my attention a few years earlier. I distinctly remembered my first visit to Phoenix. I loved it. I loved the heat, the mountains, the scenery, and the dry air. But there was something odd. One day when driving around a high-end neighborhood, I couldn't help notice there wasn't much grass. Here we were in a beautiful area with million dollar homes, and many of the yards were made of gravel. Some of them even had the rock yards painted green.

Reading about this new generation of synthetic grass and how some people were even using it in their yards, I immediately thought of Arizona. I sent Dale this simple email with a link and a thought that crossed my mind. It was a link to a backyard installation of fake grass with a few words that read, "This would be killer in the Southwest." Little did I know that this simple note with no real intention other than an anecdotal commentary would be the genesis of a multi-million dollar international business. Had I known what was to come, I might not have had the guts to send it.

A few weeks later, Dale asked if I thought any more about AstroLawn. At first, I drew a blank, and then I remembered the fake grass email.

"No, I haven't," I responded.

You'd think that would be enough to end it, but clearly it wasn't. He thought it seemed like a neat idea! We had been looking for opportunities. Working for a software consulting firm had its ups and downs. The salary was decent, we worked out of our homes, we had flexible schedules, but we had to travel, and we were continually trading time for money. We knew enough about business to know if we didn't have control of our time, someone else would. If someone else had control of our time, we weren't free and we wanted more than that. We wanted control, we wanted ownership, and most importantly, we wanted freedom.

Brian

Our father, Fred Karmie, had sought the same things. Coming from Syria as an adult, he chased the American Dream across the ocean to a new country and a new life. The American Dream Dad chased was not the dumbed down version that often sells today, filled with nothing more than a bigger home, nicer car, and more debt. Dad chased the American Dream that led to the founding of this great nation—the idea that men are "endowed by their Creator with certain unalienable Rights, that among these are Life, Liberty and the pursuit of Happiness." Our father chased freedom. Freedom to worship God as he believed and freedom to chart his own course. I think some of that was bound in our DNA. That sense of adventure and that desire to develop our God given talents to the best of our ability and be rewarded not by how much we were willing to trade, but by how much value we can provide our fellow man.

Entrepreneur; I love the word. I love the idea of risk taking and stepping out on faith. Dale and I had been kicking around various ideas of how we could jump into that ring. How could we start a business and develop that ownership? We had many ideas, but we hadn't gone too far down any of the rabbit trails. For some reason, Dale's interest had been peaked enough by the idea of artificial grass to bring it up again. He threw out the idea of giving AstroLawn a call, and I figured we had nothing to lose.

Brian

Dale

The drone of the tires on I-70 seemed the perfect accomplice to a wandering mind. Driving the highway can only garner so much of my attention, so my thoughts drifted back to that first call to AstroLawn. Robert was the person on the other end of that call. We asked basic questions: How much does it sell for? Do people really use this for their yards? How much will it cost us to buy it? What else do we need to buy for installation? How heavy is it? Are installations difficult?

How much is a dealership? Do we need a truck? So forth and so on. We gathered up answers and started building our own models. If we bought it for X, and sold it for Y, how many square feet would we need to sell to make it worthwhile? If the population were Z, what percent of the people would have to be convinced to buy our product? Where is the best opportunity for success?

We unanimously answered that last question—Phoenix. Phoenix seemed like a great combination of climate, growing population, high-income areas, and general business opportunity. We called Robert back and received our first setback in business: Phoenix was gone. At that time, we were told AstroLawn had two dealers, one in Phoenix, and one in Tampa. We were deterred, but not derailed. The excitement was fueling us. The thought of starting a business combined with the thought of moving to a new place created a nervous energy.

With Phoenix off the map, we developed a short list of possible areas where we thought the business would work—Las Vegas, Southern California, Tucson, and Orlando.

After some discussion, we felt Las Vegas would be the greatest opportunity. However, we did not want to move our families there. As crazy as it sounds, we began evaluating the idea of commuting to Las Vegas. We could sell and install during the week and fly home for the weekends. We started building our spreadsheets and doing our calculations. On paper it worked. We probably kicked that idea around for a week or two before deciding it would be too big of a toll on our families. Even if it did work for a while, at some point, we would need to move there, which we didn't want to do.

We quickly ruled out Southern California. It is a beautiful area with great weather, but it seemed too fast paced for our families. Tucson was next on the list. We liked this option. It is a smaller city, but with the desert climate, it would be a great place for artificial grass.

The Backstory

We liked the idea so much we started making calls to Tucson, trying to pre-sell the concept and judge interest. Was there as much opportunity as we expected?

I don't remember how we found it, but there was a huge housing development being built south of Tucson called Rancho Suararita. This was our first call. We contacted them and got in touch with the person responsible for development. Before we knew it, we were talking about 100,000 square feet of turf they may need, and that was just for common areas at the development. There would be 5,000 homes in the first phase, with the total number of homes to be over 15,000. If we could sell turf to even 2% of the homes (we thought that number was extremely conservative), we would have a successful business. We imagined making 100 sales in the first phase, which was $640,000 in revenue, not counting the 100,000 square feet of common area turf, which would be another $700,000 to $800,000. Our heads were spinning. In our minds, we were sitting on $1.5 million in sales on our first sales call, and we weren't even in business yet.

Never in the process did we question how we would do it. We didn't know much about artificial grass and had no practical experience in landscaping. We had never run our own business. We didn't know what that required. To us, those things were secondary details. We knew we could figure that stuff out. We would create the opportunity and then fill the need. We had done it many times before.

Brian

We have always lived "the Karmie way." When presented with a challenge or an opportunity, we accept that challenge with an unwavering conviction and a deep-seated belief that we will succeed.

Being in the computer industry, spreadsheets came naturally to us. We didn't compile overly complex sheets, just simple spreadsheets with basic formulas that could do "what if " math for us. We did some quick research, plugged in some expenses, revenues, and potential job sizes, and presto change-o, we had a profitable business (at least on computer paper). The more we played with the spreadsheets and the margins we had been discussing, the more this crazy idea started to make sense. What if this was possible? What if this was actually God directing our paths? What if we were destined for synthetic grass? What if we could just make these spreadsheets come true? While we had doubts, we didn't let those doubts overshadow the possibilities. If those numbers worked (and they surely appeared to), we knew we could figure out the rest. We always had before.

A great example of "the Karmie way" took place earlier that year in our software-consulting world. On a trip to New York City, we met with a major real estate development firm to discuss their software needs. They were looking to automate a manual process of sending out invoices and the current software didn't offer this ability. While neither Dale nor I were technically programmers, we took their needs and developed the concept of the automation solution. We had no idea how it would be done, but logically we felt it was possible. With a call to our cousin Mark, who was a programmer, and a call to our friend Danny, who was a web designer, we floated our ideas and got the feedback we needed. All we needed to hear was that it was possible. There was a good chance we could build what they wanted.

Armed with the confidence of seasoned veterans, we boldly pitched the client our vision for their solution and offered to build an electronic invoicing system that had never been used before. We committed to an aggressive timeline and a budget without knowing how we were going to deliver, but we knew if it could be done, we would figure it out. That is exactly what we did. We assembled and directed a team that had skills we didn't, and we built a system that did exactly what our client wanted it

Brian

10

to do. We did it all on time and on budget.

Don't misunderstand; we never want to over-promise and under-deliver. We always shoot for the inverse. However, we have also never let our own capabilities or lack of experience limit us. Once we know something can be done, we take calculated risks and then work hard to make the project a success. This philosophy not only worked in the computer realm, it got us started in the turf industry, and it has taken us to many new levels throughout this business venture. I believe this is a key to success at any level.

Brian

CHAPTER THREE

Did We Take a Wrong Turn at Albuquerque?

Dale

The breaking sunlight in my rear view mirror brought my attention back to the moment. We were rolling across I-70, headed west. I was now beyond tired. I tapped out from driving and Brian took over. As I wrestled to get comfortable in the passenger seat, my thoughts continued to take me back.

After the calls to Suararita, we felt we had some momentum in Tucson and we wanted to meet Theresa, the Phoenix dealer, so an in-person visit was the next step. The four of us, Brian, Angie, Lorie and I, flew out to Arizona over Memorial Day Weekend, 2002. At this point, we had been kicking around the idea of starting a turf business for about three months.

Some things in life you just can't prepare for. The heat of Phoenix and Tucson is one of those things. When we landed, it was about 110 degrees. Within minutes of stepping off the plane, Lorie announced that this wouldn't work. This was an area she wouldn't want to live because it was way too hot.

We went and met with Theresa. We were supposed to watch an install, but it was postponed because the turf didn't show up. We did get to see the grass in the ground for the first time. That was an important moment. Up to that point, all we had ever seen was our 1' square sample. Now we got beyond our imagination to seeing a completed project and it fueled our vision even more.

After a day or so in Phoenix, we made the two-hour trek down to Tucson. We may as well have been on the moon. This landscape was new to us; dry barren areas of rock, dirt, and sand, with scattered vegetation. Everything was brown. Surely, this would be a great market for artificial grass. If only we could find a way to live here.

In Tucson, we tried to meet up with our contact at Saurarita. Although he wasn't available, we did go out to look at the community. It was amazing. It was huge with thousands of homes, and most of them were in desperate need of grass. Again, our minds ran wild with the possibilities.

Brian and I were running numbers that had us making millions without ever leaving this one community. The opportunities seemed nearly limitless. However, the girls' vote was they would prefer to be somewhere, almost anywhere else, other than Tucson.

I remembered sitting in a hot tub at the hotel our last night there, and the four of us were discussing where our future would take us. At this point, the areas in discussion were Tucson, Las Vegas, Southern California, or Orlando. I think our straw poll had three predictions for Orlando, and one hold out for Tucson. We knew the opportunities would be greater in Las Vegas or Southern California, but we just couldn't imagine raising our families there. We flew back from the trip feeling confident that our future was in the turf business and pretty sure we would wind up in Florida.

A phone call when we got back home would change all of that. We called the AstroLawn corporate office and filled Robert in on the details of our trip. When we started talking about Florida, I don't think he felt that was such a good idea. Then he asked us the question that would set our course in this business and in life.

"Have you ever considered Albuquerque?" Robert asked. "We get a lot of calls from there."

"Where?"

He repeated, "Albuquerque" and stated they were imposing water restrictions so he felt it could be a good area. Brian and I got off the phone. We had just been thrown a curve ball. What would we do with it? We immediately jumped on the computer and did a search on Albuquerque.

I remember the first picture I saw of Albuquerque. It was beautiful. You could see the city with the mountains in the background. The color of the mountains was a purple hue. I had always loved mountains. Could this be the place? We started reading. We learned it got hot in the summer, but not like Phoenix. It got cold in the winter, but not really cold.

The demographics weren't as good, only 600,000 people in the metropolitan area (including outlying districts). There were a lot of lower income households, and the school systems were rated towards the bottom of the 50 states. These concerns may have deterred some people but not Brian and me; we were locked in.

As we reviewed the government website for Albuquerque, I found a section talking about water restrictions and alternate landscape ideas (to replace natural grass). I was surprised that artificial grass was not listed as an option, so I decided to send an email. Fifteen minutes later, I was hitting send on an email to the head of the water department for the Albuquerque government, explaining the benefits of artificial grass and why they should list it on their website as a landscaping alternative. While I didn't expect a response, I figured it was still worth the effort.

Brian and I came out of the office and went upstairs to where the girls were talking. We both had one of those "have I got a surprise for you" smiles on our faces that we were trying to suppress. We didn't make it all the way upstairs before one of us blurted out something like, "So what do you think about living in Albuquerque, New Mexico?"

Did We Take a Wrong Turn at Albuquerque?

Their initial reaction was much the same as ours, "Where?" After a brief discussion, they offered their approval. This had to be the hand of God directing this. In spite of a lack of knowledge or understanding of the area, we all very quickly had a comfort with pursuing the idea of moving to Albuquerque and starting a business.

The moment we shared the idea with them I had equal levels of excitement and fear running through my body. When something is verbalized, a real event happens in the mind. An idea goes beyond just an idea; it is a fledgling reality once you start to speak it and discuss it. Just like that, this Albuquerque thing had legs.

If speaking it gave it legs, the email I was soon to see gave it wings. Jean, from the Albuquerque Water Department, emailed me back. She said she was very interested in learning more about artificial turf and would like to meet with us. She also told me she would be speaking at a conference in New Orleans that next week and wanted to know if I could give her some information on turf that she could use in her presentation.

I didn't know much about artificial turf but the head of the city water department was asking me for information she could use to present to a bunch of other city department heads. There was a small crack in the door, so we decided to push it wide open. We sent Jean as much information as we could muster. We didn't have any type of marketing material, so Brian and I just started entering information into an email. We also set up a meeting with her at her office a few weeks later; we would fly to Albuquerque just to meet her.

Things were getting serious. We called Robert from the AstroLawn corporate office to see if he could fly out and join us for this meeting with the city. Things were rolling and to keep the momentum going we called other city departments; the parks department, the maintenance department, and I think a few others trying to set up meetings with them as well. In the end, we had several department heads coming to one meeting. This was good.

Brian and I scrambled. We needed business cards and brochures. We designed our own. We went up to a local print shop and had them printed out. We weren't even dealers yet. We didn't have an agreement, we hadn't signed anything, but we were moving forward. There was no sense wasting time. We could take care of that other stuff later. This mentality had been, and would continue to be, a recurring theme for us throughout our business lives.

Amidst all the excitement, I remembered that July 9 (the day we had set for our Albuquerque meeting) was my wedding anniversary. I told Lorie what our plans were. She was fine with it. I could tell, at least on some level, it hurt her that I wouldn't be spending that day with her, but she also knew what was going on and what we were trying to accomplish. She knew, as we all did, that we were following a path being laid out before us; what we believed to be an answer to prayer.

Brian

Teamwork makes the dream work. Although that statement is a bit trite, it does grow from a kernel of truth. I have no doubt that Dale and I as a team have accomplished far more together than we could have on our own. There is a synergy in a team. That is one of the reasons I love sports so much—I love teams.

The truth is Dale and I are very blessed. We have two incredible wives that are committed to us and believe in us. I can't tell you the power and freedom that gives. Looking back, I can't imagine doing what we asked our wives to do. Dale and I decided since we didn't have much startup money, our best bet was for us to go to New Mexico and try to get the business started and create some income before we moved our families out from Ohio. In the meantime, we asked Angie and Lorie to stay back in Ohio, take care of the kids, pay the bills, get our homes ready to sell, and get packed and ready to move. Did I mention that we were moving them across the country to a state that they had never visited to start a business that we knew next to noth-

16

ing about? This was no small order, but our wives did it and because of them, we have a story to tell.

I'm sure Angie and Lorie would tell you it was the grace of God that got them through, and they would be absolutely right. I also know that there is something awesome about an adventure, and they loved the chase just as we did. How else could I explain our decisions?

Angie and I were in our mid-twenties with two young daughters: Julia, 3, and Paige, just turning 2. We were a single-income family and I had recently made a large step in salary to get to a place where we were getting comfortable. Now, with no savings and no investors, we decided to give up our sole source of income and roll the dice on a cross-country move and a brand new business in an unproven industry.

Outside of providence alone, the only explanation is the excitement and romance of this adventure. Angie always liked John Wayne movies. Maybe that was part of it, the idea of taming the Wild West. In hindsight, I have trouble remembering our exact thought process, but I do remember we were focused on the good "what ifs" not the bad "what ifs." Anything new draws "what if" questions. It is up to us whether we spend more time on the positive or negative side of those questions.

No one wants to just exist. No one wants to just get by, but life happens and we react to it. Reaction is never as thrilling (nor as rewarding) as pro-action. When we chose to chart our course rather than just flowing with the current, we awoke something inside. Done wrong, an adventure like this could wreck a marriage. Done right, working together toward a common dream could pull you closer together than you've ever been. Thankfully, we chose the latter.

There was an excitement in our families as we started the

Brian

17

Brian

business. We shared a sense of adventure of what could be. We even shared a sense of destiny. Was it a struggle? Yes. Were there things we all hated? Absolutely. That wasn't what defined us though. The sense that God was doing something new and unique through us, and the excitement that we were doing it together, that is what made our team so special.

CHAPTER FOUR

Do You See What I See?

Dale

Big Blue continued to carry us westward. Every mile took us further away from what was familiar, and closer to the unknown of our new business and new home. Sitting in Blue, traveling to Albuquerque, reminded me of my first flight to visit the city just a few short months ago.

Sitting on that flight, a tingle shot up my spine as I heard the pilot's voice crackle in the speaker above me, "We are beginning our final approach into Albuquerque." I strained my neck to see out the window. To catch a glimpse of what could possibly be my new home. Would I like it? Would I hate it? Would it be a place Lorie and the kids could live?

Well, it was brown, that was for sure. But I liked it. Looking through the window, I was struck by the beauty of the mountains, at least what I could see. The many shades of brown that made up the ground were intriguing. The city appeared to be sprawling, but you could see the landscape change from homes and roads to barren desert in an instant. It was odd. It was unusual. But I liked it.

My guess is that I would have liked it no matter what it looked like. I was searching for reasons why this would work, not reasons it wouldn't. I wanted the mountains to be beautiful and the sands attractive. I wanted this to happen. This is a valuable life lesson. More than we know, our expectations and desires define our realities.

Brian and I must have looked like kids on Christmas as we walked through the airport. Anticipation was flowing out of us like water over the falls. The excitement was so high it didn't even feel like my feet were touching the floor. We couldn't stop grinning.

We grabbed our luggage and walked across the street to a hotel. We checked in and then decided to go downtown to walk around so we would be ready for the meeting the next day. We wanted to make sure we knew which building and how to get there. Funny thing was we didn't rent a car. We walked to downtown Albuquerque, which ended up being about a three-mile walk in each direction. Along the way, we saw opportunity after opportunity.

We walked by a park that had grass that was completely dead—opportunity. We saw a place with a broken sprinkler head with the water just gushing in the air—opportunity. I think on that walk, we must have identified a dozen opportunities for us to sell our grass. We were thinking enough to take pictures of the dead grass and broken sprinkler to use in our meeting the next day.

We walked the whole way to downtown and found the building where we were going to meet. It was a little anticlimactic; it was just a building downtown, but at least we knew where it was. So, we turned around and walked back. This was our introduction to Albuquerque. If someone was trying to sell a person on the idea of moving to Albuquerque, the path we walked from the airport to downtown is not the one they'd want to show. We experienced a little more of the inner city side and not the beautiful landscapes and nice homes that would entice people to move there.

Funny thing I've found when I am focused on a goal, the things on the periphery don't matter. When I want something, I get tunnel vision. We went there looking for a reason to like it. We wanted to find opportunity; we searched for it and found it. No doubt, had we gone there looking for reasons it wouldn't work, and reasons not to move there, we certainly would have found those too. Our vision and focus create our reality, not the other way around. Ultimately, my vision is developed first through prayer, then through my desires and being open to the input of people I look up to and admire.

The next morning brought several firsts. It was the first time we actually met someone from AstroLawn. It was our first official meeting where we were presenting the idea of artificial turf in person, and it was the first time we really considered Albuquerque as our "home turf."

Robert from AstroLawn was a likeable guy. He had a sports background, which Brian and I have as well, and we hit it off. We were excited to have him with us. We wanted to sit back and watch him run the meeting, so we could learn. However, we soon realized that this whole idea of artificial turf was still new. Robert was good, but there were some things we wanted said so we said them. In short, Brian and I took control of the meeting. This was another important moment for us. We had ownership. We had something at stake. We realized if things were going to happen, it was up to us, not up to someone else.

The meeting ended well, and we were certain the City of Albuquerque would be our first customer. They loved it. We spent some time driving around town (we borrowed Robert's rental car) and looked for office spaces to lease. We could feel the momentum building.

Brian

Do you remember that old Tootsie Roll commercial? You know that song, "Whatever it is I think I see, becomes a Tootsie Roll to me." I realize I'm getting a little older and only about half of those I ask still remember it (don't feel bad if you're with me—it just means you have a good memory).

But I remember it. In fact, I don't just remember it, I experienced it.

21

You see, in the commercial, little cartoon kids are running around and everything thing they look at turns into a Tootsie Roll. A boat, a baseball bat, even a whale looks like a Tootsie Roll. A little strange I guess, but the truth is our brains are like that. When something captivates your imagination, it takes over your mind. It is all you think about and all you see.

In the spring of 2002, Dale and I were becoming captivated by the thought of fake grass. One time, while consulting in New York City, I remember walking down the streets of Manhattan. Suddenly, I was the Tootsie Roll kid. Everywhere we looked we saw artificial grass! I remember Dale and I calling it out back and forth, "Oh look here! This should be grass," or "Whoa! What about the opportunity for grass at this building?" It was limitless! With no water, no mowing, no need for soil, no need for sun, so many challenges could be overcome. We could put this stuff anywhere. All we had to do was introduce people to the concept. At that moment, I knew we were in. This was it. Our future was about to be quite different from our past. I had no idea how true that was, but I knew we were about to become the fake grass guys.

A few months later, on our first trip to Albuquerque, we had this experience again. Everywhere we looked, we saw opportunity for artificial grass. It was so obvious it almost hurt. How could this not have been shouting out to anyone in this city? Everywhere was dead grass or no grass. A few splashes of green would be a perfect complement to this beautiful desert landscape.

We were like little kids giddy with excitement as we lived our own artificial grass version of the Tootsie Roll commercial. If the spreadsheets had gotten our minds running, this first visit to Albuquerque stirred our hearts.

We still have this experience when we go new places, and many

Brian

of our best dealers do too. It really is a question about vision. It's the vision of not only what is, but what could be. They often say that faith is blind, but is it? My experience has been that eyes of faith often just allow you to see what others can't (or choose not to). Often the eyes of pessimism and doubt are really the blind ones.

Dale

Upon our return home from the Albuquerque trip, we called Robert and told him we wanted to move forward with a dealership. He sent over a contract for us to review. Neither of us were attorneys, and we didn't have our own attorney, so we had to play the role. We reviewed the contract and sent Robert all of the modifications we wanted to see. He seemed surprised and said we were really supposed to just sign it. We were quite certain that the changes we suggested needed to be in the contract, so a back and forth began. Meanwhile, we started to call some of the people we had met while we were in Albuquerque.

While we didn't know how to start a business, and we didn't know much about turf, we never lacked a plan or desire. We each had a notebook where we would keep lists of companies we wanted to contact, names of people we had gathered in our visit to Albuquerque, and types of customer groups we wanted to pursue.

We also had lists of first steps. This included registering the business, supplies, tools, and money we needed to make it work. Our notebooks held the blueprint, albeit a rough one, to our future.

About this time in late July, my family took a trip to Florida with Lorie's side of the family. Amidst enjoying the pool and the sun, I was on the phone trying to get things set up for our next trip to Albuquerque.

During this vacation, I experienced something really neat. It was the feeling of freedom. I had done work on a family vacation before, but this was different. It was my work for my business, done because I wanted to do it, which was an amazing difference. It was extremely liberating.

Shortly after returning to Ohio, I received a frantic call from Brian. He let me know that a gentleman named George called him from New Mexico and informed him that he had been selling turf for AstroTurf in Albuquerque for quite some time. It literally felt like someone had just punched me right in the gut.

At that moment, we were prepared to fight for our business. We immediately called Robert at AstroLawn. He wasn't available and we somehow were connected to a new person, Andy, who was higher up in the company.

Andy was great. He started by calming us down, he listened to our story, and he assured us that Albuquerque was ours if that's what we had been told by Robert. He did a fantastic job clearing up the issue. I remember explaining to him that we were planning to leave our jobs, sell our homes, and move from Ohio to New Mexico so we could get started in this new business. He seemed surprised by this, but he encouraged us nonetheless.

Another lesson learned. Sometimes you don't know (or appreciate) what you have until someone takes it away. We pretty much knew we were going to go to Albuquerque, but we hadn't yet executed the contract because of little things here and there that really weren't that important. With the threat of losing our territory, some minor differences in the contract didn't appear as important as they had before. We were majoring on some minors and missing the big picture. That was corrected very quickly; we had tunnel vision for Albuquerque.

Brian

You know the story about the mama eagle needing to push the baby eagle out of the nest and force it to fly? Sometimes we all need that push. Dale and I were excited about this artificial grass idea. We had spreadsheets that looked good and we saw huge opportunity everywhere. We had even made a visit to Albuquerque and had what seemed like successful sales calls. We were all in. Well, kind of all in. Even with all of our excitement and vision of opportunity, we still needed that final push to cross that line once and for all; and we got it.

That final shove came from a man we never met. A man solely remembered as "Old George." Somehow George had heard we were investigating working with AstroLawn in the Albuquerque market and called to let me know this was his territory, and we needed to stop snooping around his market. I was angry. How could he say that? Had we been lied to? Was all of this going to be taken away from us? I called Dale and shared my conversation with him.

We quickly called AstroTurf and after a brief talk with Andy Belles, found George was the one mistaken, and we still had our opportunity if we were ready to move forward. That call did something. It pushed us out of our nest. Once we realized this was still ours if we wanted it, we knew we had to act now. The thought of missing this opportunity now scared us more than the challenge of the opportunity itself.

If you talk with most people later in life, you find that often the biggest regrets aren't regrets of actions taken that failed, but rather regrets of actions never taken. In our daily lives, we get so focused on the myopic view of the present and the fear of potential failure, that we miss the potential loss from inaction.

What if we feared regret as much as we feared failure? How

Brian

would that change our decisions today? Sometimes we need events to shake us just a little and cause us to look at that potential loss and give us a fear of regret. I'm thankful we had an event like that with the call from our buddy "Old George."

CHAPTER FIVE

Either We're in or We're out

Dale

"We're low on gas. We need to stop and fill up." I heard Brian exclaim as he hit the blinker and guided Big Blue toward the exit ramp.

For us, getting low on fuel was a good thing. It forced us to stop, stretch, and shake off the highway blues. We filled the tank, grabbed ourselves some drinks and jerky, then climbed back in the cockpit and headed back out on I-70. It didn't take more than a couple of miles for me to get back into reflection mode—I thought about our second trip to Albuquerque.

That was the trip we stuck our flag in the ground and claimed Albuquerque as our home. Up until that point, we knew this was what we wanted to do and we were moving forward, but we still had a back door. We didn't have to leave Ohio. We didn't have to commit to Albuquerque; we still had an escape hatch we could use. But on trip number two, we realized our commitment in an unlikely place. We found ourselves walking through a mall and looking around a cell phone shop. The salesman jumped right in to help us by trying to sell us a phone. My defenses immediately went up, like a boxer trying to protect himself from the blows of the opposition.

"I don't need a phone," I explained. "I already have one."

As I attempted to logic my way out of the sale, we somehow realized that while we had phones, we didn't have an Albuquerque number. How could we sell grass in New Mexico with an Ohio phone number? Conviction washed over me—we couldn't. Brian and I stared at each other, almost silently. We were both thinking the same thing, but neither one of us seemed to have the courage to act. We needed new phones.

After some banter back and forth, we somehow convinced each other we could get one phone, and if we didn't end up moving to Albuquerque, we could return it or cancel the number. We were trying to keep our escape options open. Decisions are often easier to make if you think you can hedge the bet. We got the phone. Funny thing, as soon as it was activated, and we held it in our hand, we knew what we had done. We hadn't just purchased a new cell phone plan; we had just started our new business, and claimed Albuquerque as our new home.

Brian

Dale and I have always had a great relationship. When we were working for the same software consulting firm, we lived about an hour apart in Northeast Ohio. We talked daily about work and family and saw each other at least once a week. One spring day in 2001, I was in Southern California working with a client. I finished up a little early and decided to check in with Dale who happened to be visiting a client in the Bay Area. He had a little free time as well.

While we were about 400 miles apart and I had to catch a flight in the morning, we decided to meet in the middle and grab dinner together.

Six hours of driving in an unknown area for a steak dinner. This kind of summarizes Dale and me. We've always enjoyed time together and had a sense of adventure. So, in one sense, this adventure wasn't new, but this time the stakes were much bigger than a 10-ounce ribeye.

This wasn't just a fun trip; this adventure was a change in the course of our lives. We were stepping out on faith and making a commitment to each other and to our families. We'd never done anything quite like this, but when we made the commitment, we weren't turning back.

Commitment is a scary thing, but often the best things in life lay on the other side of commitment. Sports teams have to commit to each other and to a common goal in order to be successful. Marriages and the special blessing they offer are begun with a commitment "from this day forward..."

While part of me felt like Lloyd Christmas (from the movie *Dumb and Dumber*) saying, "We're really doing it Harry!" as we drove across the country, there were also moments of silence, prayer, and some somber reflection. We had moved from idea to launch quickly, but we didn't take this lightly. We were committed.

Brian

Dale

Usually a long highway trip can become very mundane and monotonous. Not this one. Every mile passed was another step in our journey. Questions darted through my head. What was ahead of us? Could we do it? Did we have what it took to start a new business in an area we had never been and in a business arena we really knew nothing about?

Brian and I never felt we had to have all the answers before moving forward. We could figure out the details. I've heard it said that you can't steer a parked car. We certainly weren't a parked car—we put it in drive, and hammered the gas, trusting that we could figure it out and make course corrections as we went.

Somewhere near St. Louis, Brian and I decided we needed to call our current employer and let them know a little of what was going on. Since we were consultants, we figured we could work from New Mexico the same as we could from Ohio. In any event, this was not a call we wanted to make.

Brian dialed Steve's number. With any luck, he would get his voice mail and could leave him a cryptic message. No luck. Steve answered the phone.

"Hey Steve, this is Brian. I just wanted to check in and let you know I'd be out of the office for a little while. How long? Oh, I don't know maybe a few weeks. Dale and I decided to take a trip to Albuquerque." Shaking his head in agreement, "Yes, Albuquerque, New Mexico. Well, I guess you could say it's a couple of brothers taking a bonding trip, hitting the open road. Oh yes, we brought our computers and will be doing some work from the road. We'll let you know if we need anything. Hey, if you need to reach us, just call our cell."

Whew! We were glad when that call was over. It was awkward, and I think it left Steve with more questions than answers. While we didn't offer full disclosure, we also did not lie or make up stories about going somewhere else, trying to cover our tracks. If you tell the truth, you never have to remember what you said. If you lie, then you have to remember the lie and build off it, and a web of deceit will ultimately trap you.

I made calls home to check in on Lorie and the kids. I had left Derek, Kaylyn, and Makenna with a map of the U.S., and told them they could track our progress as we went. I remember calling to tell them I had seen the St. Louis Arch. I told them I missed them, and they said the same. It was difficult to make small talk. Every time I called them, the pit in my stomach felt like it was the size of a basketball. What could I say? I miss you and I love you pretty much covered it.

As we neared Oklahoma, the doubts crept back in my mind. Had we really thought this through? Was I doing the right thing leaving my family behind? Each set of questions seemed to bring another set of questions. How long would I be able to juggle software consulting and the start of our new business? Would Lorie be able to keep her spirits up without me there? Where would our money come from? Hundreds of questions flooded my mind. The problem was I didn't have the answers. Only time would tell.

I looked over at Brian and asked the question I'm sure we both wanted to ask but neither of us wanted to say out loud. I figured we were past the point of no return if we didn't come up with the answer we needed.

"Are we doing the right thing? I mean, we are leaving our families and homes behind to move across the country, to a place we don't know. We are essentially quitting our jobs and putting all of our eggs in this one basket. Do you really think we are making the right move?"

"Well, I sure hope so," Brian said flatly with a small grin on his face.

As we talked through it and recounted what we were doing and what had brought us to this point, we settled on these key points:

1. As Christian men, we had spent much time in prayer over this and clearly felt this was where God was leading us. If we were right about that, then this was the correct move.

2. As couples, we had gone over this decision a dozen different times. We knew we needed to change what we were doing as far as our vocation. We were open to moving, and we were open to risks.

3. We wanted to do something new and exciting – not much doubt about that one.

4. We wanted to be involved in something where we could positively impact those around us. This was a little less clear, but we still felt we had a better chance to do that in our own business, than by working for someone else.

So, somewhere in Oklahoma, in the quiet of night, with the scattered lights of the oncoming cars painting our faces, we reaffirmed that what we were doing was good and right.

CHAPTER SIX

Just Fall Forward

Dale

We continued rolling on toward New Mexico. As we drove on, I thought back to our second trip to Albuquerque again. Yes, we had purchased a phone, but we had taken a few lumps on that trip too. We had set up some meetings with bankers to try and get financing for our new business.

It's a sick feeling to be sitting in front of a banker listening to him explain how our business idea was flawed. That was what we had to sit through on that second trip in August of 2002. He sat behind a big cherry desk having no ownership experience, yet he had no problem pointing out all the reasons we wouldn't be successful, and therefore, why he wouldn't loan us the money. To add insult to injury he even laughed at our idea and at us.

As I listened to him put us down, anger burned inside of me. We don't have to take this, do we? I wanted to yell at him, to tell him how stupid he was. Knowing this would not accomplish anything, I just sat there and nodded as he spoke. We offered a few rebuttals, but they fell on deaf ears and we were ushered out the door.

I remember getting in the car and driving off and neither Brian nor I said anything. What was there to say? We certainly didn't want to relive the meeting. Then one of us broke the silence asking the question; What if he is right and this wouldn't work? We kicked around all the doubt. We were both downhearted. As we talked through it, we came to realize just the opposite. It wasn't that the banker knew something we didn't; it was that we knew something the banker didn't. We knew our resolve. We knew we could make it work. We knew where we were being led. We knew we were on the right path.

We threw off the shackles he tried putting on us and continued on. Unfortunately, the next meeting with a banker later that same day ended the same way. This time, however, the banker's doubt became fuel for our fire. It simply strengthened our resolve.

"We'll show them," Brian said as we walked out of that second bank. "We don't need their money. We will do it on our own."

Times like this pointed out how important Brian was to me. He always stepped up when I was down. We shared ideas. We sharpened each other but the biggest thing he did for me was to encourage me and keep me moving forward.

Although our visits to the bank were unsuccessful, the whole trip didn't have to be. We found a couple of potential spaces we could lease, made our sales calls, and of course, got our phone. That is a valuable lesson we learned. You don't win every battle, but even if you lose one, you can work to salvage something else. It's ok to fall; you just have to fall forward.

When we got back to Ohio we all lamented the fact that we couldn't get a loan to finance the business, but at the same we time determined that obviously that wasn't supposed to happen. The money would come to us another way. God would provide as He always had. We set a date. September 25, 2002. That was the day the lease would start on our office space. Everything kicked into high gear. We put our homes up for sale. We started looking for a truck and trailer. We were only about four weeks away from leaving. How could we get it all done?

Brian

Thinking back, it had to be either that beauty is in the eye of the beholder or that vision sees what could be rather than what is. The truth is it really was just an ugly 1'x1' piece of black plastic sheeting with some green strands coming out of the top. By the standard of today's ForeverLawn products, I'd be ashamed to show it. By weight, it literally is less than 1/3 of the product that we offer today and far less than that in realism. Yet in 2002, it was gorgeous—just what my sore eyes needed to see. It didn't just look like grass, it looked like opportunity. It looked like a doorway to something beyond where we were.

Sometimes, I wonder what everyone else really thought. I remember throwing that grass square out whenever we were around friends and family. I'd toss it in the grass and say, "See! Look how it blends in." Maybe if the light was right, the real grass was wet, and we were far enough away, others would see what I did, but in all honesty, this single color lightweight plastic grass wasn't fooling anyone.

I specifically remember showing it to my father-in-law, Steve. Steve is a good man who is very supportive. He grew up on a farm. The idea of selling plastic grass had to strike a hard working Midwestern man more than just a little bit odd. I remember him asking if I really thought people would do their whole yards with it, but when I told him about the painted gravel, he just shook his head and encouraged us. I'm sure in his heart he was conflicted. Here was this young 20-something kid who was planning to take his daughter and only two grandchildren 2,000 miles across the country, all for chasing this little square of plastic.

I learned something then. We did have the naysayers, or the "crabs in the bucket" trying to pull us back in with them, but we were blessed that those closest to us were supportive. They may not have seen exactly what we saw, but they saw our passion and believed in us. There is something about somebody on fire that burns right through opposition. Discouraging comments bounce off, but those who know you well, and have eyes of faith, encourage. I think about this sometimes now when people bring ideas to me that seem a little crazy. I have no issues with a reality check. I have no problem with using logic to work through some pros and cons. However, any time I get close to dumping a full-blown bucket of water on an idea, I remember where we were with the square piece of turf and I do my best to see with eyes of faith and encourage.

I read a story one time about how mountain climbers couldn't achieve their climb if they didn't have someone holding the rope for them. The rope holder may not be able to be out on every peak, but without them, the mission couldn't be a success. We've had many rope holders throughout our entrepreneurial adventures. Our older brothers, Jim and Ken, have sometimes held the rope, and other times swung out on the ropes with us. Our Mom and Dad raised the four of us to be close. True to our family values, Jim and Ken were with us in one way or another through the entire journey.

Jim was there when we made that first call to AstroLawn and started our spreadsheets. He shared our excitement, and while moving his family wasn't in the cards when we decided to head west, he helped us explore the idea and supported us all the way.

When it became evident that Albuquerque was eminent, Ken offered a sounding board and a little bit of perspective. He asked some good honest questions on our plans. Some of those questions we had good answers to and some we just blew past in our enthusiasm. Unlike doubters who try to poke holes in your balloon as you are trying to take off, Ken wasn't a naysayer, he was an encourager.

We are very blessed to have the family that we do. We were raised on values of faith and hard work. We had a father who set a great example of chasing dreams and being willing to do whatever it takes. We had a mother who taught us unconditional love and the servant mindset of thinking of others higher than ourselves. We had brothers that were best friends and iron that sharpens iron. All of these were vital to preparing us for this venture.

Brian

CHAPTER SEVEN

Home Sweet Home?

Dale

The fact that we were closing in on our destination couldn't overcome the overwhelming feeling of sheer exhaustion. My blinks were growing longer. I was fighting to keep our truck between the white lines. As determined as I was, I needed to shake it up. I needed to talk. A funny story sure would help.

I got Brian's attention.

"Hey, remember that call with Bic? Now that was funny." That got us both chuckling as we relived that recent call.

Bic was one of the few leads we had received from AstroLawn prior to the move. He had filled out an online form, and his information was passed on to us. Brian called him from Ohio to introduce us and answer any questions he might have. As they talked about the products, Brian began to explain to Bic about the infill we used on the products. He told him how we put crumb rubber in the grass by spreading it on the grass, then brooming it in-between the blades. This helps to support the grass blades and helps with the underfoot feel.

Considering we hardly knew what we were saying, Brian was doing really well. Then Bic asked, "Well how much infill do you put into the product?"

Brian confidently replied, "About two pounds per square inch." This was funny, because the correct answer should have been two pounds per square foot. Bic seemed surprised by Brian's answer and said, "I think you mean per square foot."

Brian retorted, "No, it's definitely two pounds per square inch."

After this went back and forth a couple of times, Bic finally said, "I'm looking at a square inch, and I don't see how you could get two pounds of anything into a square inch."

As Bic was saying this, Brian made a square inch with his fingers and had the immediate realization that Bic was right; it was two pounds per square foot. Brian and I laughed and laughed at that. Every time we'd recount Bic trying to figure out how we'd get two pounds of anything into a square inch, we would just start laughing all the more. It may have been our tired state, but that story entertained (and awakened) us for many miles.

Amidst the humor though, this story demonstrates our move forward mentality. We didn't have to know everything (and we didn't). We made mistakes. We admitted that we didn't know things. However, we spoke to people with confidence and we took action. That is the engine that drove our business.

As we drove down the final stretch of the Texas panhandle, closing in on New Mexico, I thought a little more about what we were doing. We were starting a new business; we were moving to a strange new land. We really had no road map to follow. We had to create our own marketing material. We pulled a few pictures off the Internet of turf installations and dumped them into a Word document. We added some nice text and we had a marketing sheet. We were smart enough to know better than to print it ourselves, so we took it to a printer to have it printed professionally. We also had the forethought to have some yard signs (to promote the jobs once they were completed) and business cards printed. Those pieces, and the few supplies we were pulling behind us, completed our arsenal to start our own business.

As the dawn was breaking in the eastern sky behind us, there we were, crossing the border from Texas to New Mexico—our new home. All the memories that had been flooding my mind, all of the recounting what had brought us to this point, all the hours of preparation, all the calls and planning, all the events of the past seven months were coming to fruition in this moment as we crossed the state line. I know it is somewhat of an arbitrary line, an invisible border between states, marked only by a road sign that read, "Welcome to New Mexico," but this sign was different and the event big. It was as if we were crossing a threshold. My spine was tingling and the hair stood up on the back of my neck. We had entered the new land. We both knew in that moment that our lives had changed and our fortunes, families, and future hung in the balance. It was a surreal moment.

As the cloak of the nighttime darkness lifted off the landscape around us, the new terrain came into view. It was rocky with scattered shrubs and yucca plants. It was mostly flat, but we could begin to see the mountains in the far off distance. Funny, as I looked around, I could very easily envision the Road Runner from the old Looney Tunes Cartoon cruising around trying to escape the Coyote. Other than our two trips to Albuquerque, that was about the extent of my exposure to the New Mexican terrain. Although somewhat barren, and completely different from Ohio, it had its own unique allure, a different kind of beauty. I wondered if it would ever feel like home to me.

The highway cut through the Sandia Mountains and descended down to Albuquerque. As we came through the pass, we could see the city sprawl out beneath us. We made it. It was about 9:00 a.m. on Tuesday morning, September 24, 2002. We had been in the truck for about 30 hours now, and other than a few hours on the side of the road, and some naps while the other was driving, we hadn't slept since Saturday night.

Home Sweet Home?

We were tired, dirty, and were really in need of a shower and a bed. The catch was we didn't have anywhere to go. In an effort to save money (or better stated, due to a lack of money) we had determined we would live in the warehouse to get started. So we had to head to the real estate office to pick up the keys to the warehouse. Our lease didn't start until October 1, but we had arranged with Mr. Williams, the landlord, to get into the space a week early.

We pulled our truck and trailer into the parking lot of the office building on Louisiana Avenue. It is hard to maneuver and park something like this in a normal parking lot, so we worked our way to the backside of the building, and parked along the back curb. We looked at each other and said, "Let's go get this started."

While we had agreed to the terms of the office space, the lease had not been signed. Mr. Williams had been asking for our income statement and balance sheet the last week or so before we left Ohio. We didn't have anything, since we hadn't started our business yet, and hadn't made any money. We hadn't told him this, but somehow I think he got the impression we were moving our business from somewhere else to Albuquerque. So, in lieu of sending him our financials, we had told him we would get him something once we got to town. As we prepared to walk into the building to meet him, to actually sign the lease and get the keys, we were a little tentative. How would he react? Would we still be able to get into the space?

Oh well, we had gotten this far so we headed inside. As we walked up the stairs on the backside of the building, we paused to look out the window at our truck and trailer. As we did, it struck us both how ragtag it looked. We had a pickup truck with the bed of the truck just stuffed with things like a dresser, boxes, shovels, and a day bed with a little mattress. The trailer had a motorcycle, more lawn tools, boxes, a couch, a few chairs, a desk, and some other stuff. It looked like the Beverly Hillbillies had rolled into town.

We looked at the rig, then at each other, and just started laughing. It took us a minute or so in the stairwell to compose ourselves. We hoped Mr. Williams hadn't seen us pull in.

Our hopes that maybe he wouldn't be in, and that we could have his secretary hand us the lease to sign and give us the keys, were quickly dashed. He was there and he didn't disappoint. He asked for the financials. We told him we had just rolled into town and didn't have all that stuff prepared yet, but we would get it to him. He seemed a little concerned, but accepted that. We hadn't planned on the next question.

"Where are you guys staying?" Mr. Williams asked.

We certainly didn't want anyone knowing we were planning to live in the warehouse. We were both caught off guard and really didn't know how to respond to this. We kind of mumbled our way around that one, and hinted that we would be at a hotel until we found something permanent.

After a little more small talk and signing the lease, we got the keys and headed toward our new home.

Brian

It was 2,000 square feet of prime real estate. Well, almost prime. Well, not too bad. Ok, it was kind of a worn out old strip plaza. Anyway, it was worth it. We knew we needed a good home base for our business if we were going to develop the business of our dreams, so our first location had to fit the bill. It had some office space, some warehouse space, and even some living quarters. In between the front office and the back warehouse was a place I called Middle Earth. It was a 12' x 10' area right off the 4' x 6' bathroom. We used it for storage and sleeping quarters. We had left our families and homes in Ohio and hated to spend the little money we had on hotels, especially when we had already spent so much money on this office lease.

We weren't bold enough to put a full bedroom suite in Middle Earth, but we did bring one old daybed that Angie's grandmother had given to us before we left Ohio. We tried our best to pass it off as a couch, and we'd stuff our pillows and blankets underneath the daybed during the day. Every night we'd trade—one of us on the day bed, and the other on the couch or concrete floor. Not the best, but it could have been worse. In reality, the sleeping arrangements weren't nearly as bad as the bathing arrangements. All we had was a small bathroom sink and a one-gallon hot water tank. In those conditions, there is only so much you can do to clean up after a long day of installing turf. It wasn't exactly what we had dreamed of, but it allowed us to take money we would have spent on our comfort and reinvest it back into our business. When you start a business with no real cash on hand, you need every penny.

We did our best to hide our living arrangements from our business neighbors. I'm pretty sure it was against code, and certainly wouldn't create the impression of an up and coming business. However, when your truck is always there overnight, I think a few people caught on.

Then we had the open house.

Our next-door business neighbors had worked with the Chamber of Commerce to host an after-hours event and a ribbon cutting ceremony. Since they were short on space, and our warehouse was fairly empty at the time, we agreed to let them use our warehouse section to set up tables for the event. The day of the event, we did our best to clean up Middle Earth. We dressed the daybed up in its finest couch clothing and made the area look as un-lived in as possible. There were many visitors

Brian

43

that day streaming through both offices. The party spread from our neighbors to our space and eventually took over our entire suite. I'm not sure the total number of visitors, but I know the guest list included area business leaders and even our Congresswoman. I also remember more than one guest inquiring about the bed, as they'd walk through Middle Earth. At first, I tried covering by telling them it was actually a couch, but that got old quick. I decided the best option was just to stay away from that area and let them make their own best guesses.

Every now and then, we'd splurge for a room at the Inn-town Suites so we could cook some food and take a few showers. Oh, the luxury of both of us having a bed with a mattress and being able to shower rather than splash ourselves from the sink. Not to mention the TV and a kitchen area. What a luxury! We'd only do that for a couple of nights and then back to Middle Earth.

Our training manual was a roll of turf. Literally. AstroLawn was just getting started, so there really wasn't much experience to share, mostly theory. We didn't have any written instructions on how to install and definitely no hands on training. We had a couple phone conversations with the guys at the headquarters, and then we received our roll of turf.

There was a small 5' x 17' area between the sidewalk and the street in front of our office. We decided this would be a great place to install a showpiece and hone our skills. We measured the area, smoothed and compacted the base, and got the area ready for its makeover. Dale and I rolled out the turf in our warehouse, cut what we needed, and carried it up to the front. As we unrolled the turf, there was a sense of pride seeing that area turn from brown to green. Instant lawn—what a concept!

I grabbed the end and pulled it down toward my edge of the

Brian

sidewalk area, looking good. At the other end, Dale started tugging a little too hard and pulled my side right off the edge. After about two or three rounds of this tug of war, we realized that we had cut it about 1' shorter than it needed to be. We had missed our very first cut! We looked at it for a little bit and debated how to make it work. Since we had already decided that we were going to avoid seaming multiple pieces of turf together (I mean no one really has a need for an area bigger than 15' wide anyway, right?), we did the only logical thing. We went to Lowe's, bought a few paver bricks, and filled in the side where the turf was cut short. Presto! All better.

It is somewhat funny now, but at the time, there was a sense of concern over botching our first install, especially since it was a simple little rectangle in front of our office. The truth is, we didn't fail, we learned. Sometimes there is no substitute for experience. Sometimes Nike is right: you have to "Just Do It." This install was small, not the best looking, and we missed our first cut, but we did it. We had started. It may have been our first installation mistake, but it wouldn't be our last. If we had let the fear of the mistake prevent us from trying, we'd have prevented many mistakes, but would have prevented many successes as well. Game on.

Brian

CHAPTER EIGHT

Foundations Forged in Mud

Dale

I'm not sure how long I thought it should take to sell our first job, but after being open for about three weeks, we still had not sold anything. When you don't have much money, a few weeks without a job are tough. Then one day we received a call at our office from a guy named Charlie in Santa Fe. He wanted an estimate on his backyard. He seemed very interested on the phone, and seemed to know what he wanted. The few estimates we had done to this point we had done together, but Brian had flown off for a short consulting gig, so I was running this one alone.

Since money was tight, and the estimate was in Santa Fe (about 40 miles away), I decided to take my motorcycle up. I found Charlie's house and parked the bike at the end of the driveway. I didn't want him to see the motorcycle—it didn't seem professional enough. I didn't want him thinking we weren't a real business. As I got off the bike and removed my helmet and gloves, I watched a car drive up the road and pull into the driveway. It was Charlie.

Charlie was a nice guy. We talked briefly and then I went out to measure the yard. He had a few areas to address that included a backyard section against the house and a terrace that was up at a different level. On the terrace, he wanted a putting green with fringe around it.

This was all new to me. It was probably only the third or fourth estimate we'd done, and this one included a putting green. I took all the measurements, asked Charlie a few questions, and told him I would get back to him. Aside from the motorcycle, I worked hard to present a professional and seasoned image. Charlie asked if we had done other jobs.

"Of course," I said. "You've probably heard of the McLeod Commercial Plaza in Albuquerque. We installed the grass in the front of that plaza."

Charlie didn't seem to recognize the name. Not surprising since I had kind of made it up. The McLeod Commercial Plaza was the little retail strip our office was in. The job I was referring to was the small 5' x 17' piece of turf we had installed (incorrectly, I might add) in front of the building. I let Charlie search his memory for just a moment, and quickly moved on to talking about the benefits of our turf. I assured him I would get back to him, as he appeared to be in a hurry to get this done, and off I went.

A couple days later, I called Charlie with the proposal. When I gave him the price, he asked if we could get it down any. I told him it was a pretty good price already, considering the stone base and everything. He then came up with the idea that he didn't need the stone base. He told me his dirt was hard and we could just compact the dirt and put the grass over that. That should save us some time and money.

I didn't know a lot about installs. I had never really done one, aside from the small piece out front, but I did know that there was supposed to be a stone base. I told him I really thought he would need the stone base. He assured me he wouldn't and asked what the price would be without it. I did a few quick calculations and gave him the number, but reiterated that he would really want the base.

When he heard the new number without the base, he didn't hesitate, "I'll do it," Charlie said.

"Wow," I thought. "What should I do?" I was pretty sure not using a base was a bad idea. However, Charlie was very confident in his hard soil being fine. Additionally, there was a job on the line, our first job!

I relented and agreed.

We had our first sale. I was excited! No, elated! If we could sell one, we could sell more. This was really going to work. However, I was also scared. I was scared about not doing a stone base. I was scared about doing an install. I was worried that if we didn't do it well, we may never get another job. Everyone would know how bad we did. It was an odd range of emotions.

One week later, as we prepared for our first job, we realized we had a conundrum. We had the turf, we had the spikes we needed to secure it, but we had no idea how to do seams. We didn't have any seam tape and we didn't have any glue. When we were ordering the grass, we didn't think about it.

We decided our best bet was to check out a carpet supply place. We stopped at one on the way to Charlie's house. When we got there, we told the guys we needed outdoor glue that would work with synthetic grass. They had no idea what we were talking about. They asked if it was similar to indoor/outdoor carpet. We guessed that it was. We did know that the backing was urethane, so we told them that and they brought us a bucket of glue. We then asked about seam tape. All they had was self-adhesive carpet tape. We knew that wasn't right, but it was all they had, so we got it and headed to Charlie's.

Day One

The backyard was dirt. It was a small area that was closed in by an adobe wall about 3' high. There was an 8' x 8' cement patio, and the yard came from the house, out around the patio, with the far end of the yard toward the wall having trees along it. Since the area was already barren, and we weren't putting down any gravel, we figured we would start right in with the compacting (or tamping). The only tamper we had was an 8" by 8" metal hand tamper with a wooden handle. We were going to tamp about 400 square feet by hand, eight inches square at a time.

We had been told that when tamping gravel, the gravel needed to be wet with water so it would compact. We weren't using gravel, but figured water would help the dirt compact.

This being our first install, we had hoped beyond hope Charlie wouldn't be there. We knew there might be a few struggles and it would be better to get through them while he was at work. Unfortunately, we had no such luck. Charlie took the day off work and he was what we affectionately refer to as a "hawk-eye." He was outside, right beside us. He watched everything we did and listened to everything we said.

He heard our discussion about using water to compact the dirt and when we decided to wet the area, Charlie got the hose and turned on the water. Brian took the hose and began wetting the dirt as I pounded the ground with the hand tamper. Quickly we realized this was a bad idea. The ground, which was dirt, immediately turned to mud. The mud stuck to the tamper as I pounded the ground. In less than a minute, the end of my tamper was a giant ball of mud, and every impression I made with the tamper left an uneven, clumpy, muddy surface.

I gave Brian the cancel sign with my hand. As he turned his body to shut off the hose at the spigot, he forgot to release the hose handle, so the water was still spraying. It continued to spray—all over Charlie. He had headed over to shut off the water as Brian turned to do the same. It would have been comical if I weren't so terrified. Brian seemed confused, just kind of standing there, spraying Charlie with the hose. In reality, it was only one or two seconds, but it seemed like an eternity that Brian blasted Charlie with the water. After the water was finally turned off, we just stared at Charlie who now stood in dress shirt and pants, soaking wet.

We offered up our sincerest apologies to Charlie. He was good spirited and took it in stride. So, with the idea of tamping now out of the question, we figured we'd start laying down the grass. With the wall

all around the yard, we didn't have enough room to roll out the grass, so we decided to measure the area, roll out and cut the grass in the driveway, roll it back up, bring it into the yard and then lay it out.

We measured the distance from the wall up the side of the patio. Charlie was like a crewmember helping us measure the area. We recorded what direction the end of the patio went and recorded the length so we could make the right cut on the corner. Remembering our mistake installing the turf in front of our office, we measured everything at least three times. We were confident that we had it right.

Down in the driveway, we rolled out the turf. We then flipped it over (grass side down) so we could cut the grass easily from the back. We figured out how it was laying, picked a starting point, and began to plot all the key points we needed to cut the grass. We measured and marked, then measured again to make sure all was right. Charlie was right there watching.

After cutting, we rolled up the grass so we could take it into the backyard. This is where we ran into a few problems. This was the first roll of grass Brian and I had ever carried into a yard. When we rolled it up after cutting, we did not use the center tube. Therefore, the roll had no rigidity. We also neglected to turn the grass over, and rolled it up with the grass blades on the outside. I got on one end to lift, Brian on the other, and when we lifted, the middle just stayed on the ground. Charlie saw our problem and sprang into action.

The grass has no handles, and it is hard to grasp in the middle, so Charlie maneuvered himself under the grass and kind of lifted the middle with his back. Off we went. The next problem came when we had to go through not one, but two gates to get into the backyard. The short area in-between also included a 90-degree turn. So now, in addition to trying to move the roll, which is both heavy and awkward, we had to make our way through double gates with a right angle turn.

As we pushed and pulled, trying to shove through the gates, the grass began to both twist and uncoil. It was like wrestling a 15' long boa constrictor. Charlie appeared to be getting tired and was all hunched over with the grass on his back. We had worked our way to the second gate and were now coming into the yard on the front end, but were still stuck in the gates on the back end. It felt like a tug of war.

We were almost through but were hung up on the gate. We gave a final push and were able to dislodge the grass. The push sent the grass bursting into the backyard, and the sudden movement simultaneously knocked poor Charlie to the ground and dislodged my grip from the back end of the grass.

Charlie was on the ground. Yes, there he was on the wet and muddy ground with a twisted roll of grass on his back. As I looked at our tired, sweaty, and now muddy customer struggling on the ground, I couldn't help but wonder how he would react. We quickly got the grass off Charlie and got him to his feet. To his credit, he did not lose his temper. He kind of chuckled a little and began wiping himself off.

What had started as a nicely rolled piece of grass in the driveway was now a twisted, bent, partially unraveled piece of turf lying in the mud. Also, since we had cut it from behind and then rolled it up, the grass blades were facing out and were catching all the mud. Unrolling this twisted mess was not easy. After fighting with it for about 10 minutes, we finally got it opened.

Odds were it would not be laying the right direction, since we had forgotten which side needed to fit around the patio we weren't surprised when the grass cut did not match up immediately.

"We just need to turn it 90 degrees," I said confidently.

Brian and Charlie agreed, so we turned it. However, after turning it, we could see that it still wasn't the right cut or right fit.

"Better turn it another 90 degrees," Brian chimed in. So, we turned it again, but it still wasn't right.

We turned it another 90 degrees—not right. Then another 90 degrees—not right, and as we were calling for yet another 90 degrees, we realized we had already tried every side of the grass we could try.

"Huh," Brian mumbled. "That's odd."

"Maybe we cut it wrong," Charlie quipped.

As we pondered this perplexing situation, it dawned on me that although we had painstakingly measured and marked the correct cuts, we had done so on the back of the grass. Since the grass was upside down when we marked it, we in reality marked everything backwards.

It only went downhill from there. We had to cut the grass into parts and seam it back together. As we were putting the seams together, the grass wouldn't stick to the glue or tape. We were trying to hide this problem from Charlie, but we really began to sweat because we had to get these seams together. Upon further inspection of the glue label, we found we were sold glue that was NOT to be used with polyurethane. The problem was that our grass backing was urethane. It was repelling like oil and water.

We had to adapt on the fly, forego the use of glue, and use spikes all along the seams to hold them together. As we struggled through the install, day turned to night. We were up against a deadline because we were flying home in two days for our first return trip to see our families. So, Charlie broke out a flashlight and held it for us as we cut the turf and put it into place in his yard.

As I was attempting to cut along a diagonal edge along the back wall (which is a difficult cut), Brian encouraged me to be careful with the cut and not cut it short.

"Don't worry; I know what I'm doing," I replied.

With that, I pulled my knife across the back of the grass, and the knife continued right across the pointer finger on my other hand. I instantly knew it was a pretty bad cut.

I didn't want Charlie to see the blood, so I made a fist trapping the finger in the center, trying to stop the bleeding. Fortunately, at the same moment Charlie got a phone call in the house. Brian and I found a piece of material off the edge of the grass and wrapped my finger. Then, as we went back to the grass, we realized not only did I hack my finger, I had hacked the cut. We decided enough was enough at that point and called it a night. We found a nice big piece of scrap turf and we laid it over the botched cut in hopes that Charlie wouldn't see it. That was the end of day one of our first install.

Day Two

The best thing about day two on the install was Charlie didn't stay home. After our experience with the base in his back yard, we determined that we really needed to use gravel for a base under the putting green. Since we hadn't quoted that in the price, we told Charlie he would need to order some. He didn't want to, so he told us we could take decorative gravel out of his front yard and use it for the base.

This presented three problems. One, decorative gravel is not a good stone base. Two, his front yard was about 70 yards or more from his backyard, and to get from one to the other was a complete obstacle course. We had to maneuver along a skinny path, over a small wall, through a few gates, across the backyard, and up a set of steps to the terrace. Three, we didn't have a wheelbarrow.

For the first half of the day, we shoveled gravel in the front yard into five-gallon plastic buckets and carried them one in each hand across the obstacle course to the terrace. Once we finally had all the gravel up there, we realized we didn't have a power tamper to compact the base. We called Charlie at work and amazingly, he had one in his garage. We fished it out, but shortly after we got it started, it stopped working. We discovered that the fuel hose split. Just as we were sitting there taking the fuel hose off trying to fix it, Charlie showed up. I am sure from the appearance he thought that we had broken the tamper.

We finally got the area tamped and were able to layout the putting green material and the fringe around it, but none of it was cut. We went home exhausted.

That night, as we lay there trying to sleep, stinky and sweaty, we were startled to hear a strange sound on the roof. It was the sound of rain. We fretted on how this may affect our job and if the turf would wash away or still be there in the morning. Eventually we dozed off amidst our worries and a heavy downpour.

Day Three

We were happy to find out that the grass was where we left it when we arrived the next morning. We went to work cutting the grass for the putting green and getting it all put together. We were racing the clock because we were flying home to see our families that evening. When we finally got everything done, we took a step back and looked at it. Despite all the problems and struggles, it looked pretty darn good.

We called Charlie out so he could see the job, approve of it, and get us our check. Charlie walked up to the terrace, looked at the putting green, and asked one simple question, "Where are the holes?"

"The holes?" I said, "Oh! The holes!"

We had installed the green, but somehow never considered that a putting green needed holes and cups. We danced around on this issue. We told him the putting cups hadn't come in with the order and we would come back up and install them as soon as they came in. Plus, he could putt on the green and play the breaks, and then he could determine where he wanted the cups.

He was very happy with the project overall, and he wrote us the check for the completed job. As he wrote out the check and handed it to Brian, I tried to hide in the trees and take a picture. Our first check! Our first paying customer! We had done it!

We got in the truck and immediately started hammering it toward Albuquerque. We were about an hour away from the airport and our flight was to leave in about an hour and twenty minutes. We prayed, "God, please don't let us miss this flight."

As we drove down the road, we began recounting the events of the last three days. With the job done and the customer happy, we were able to relax a little, and the humor of the events finally hit us. We told the stories and laughed. We laughed hard, so hard I couldn't breathe, and tears were streaming down my face. It was one funny story after the next.

"Let's call Ken," Brian said. "He'll never believe what just happened."

So, the hour trip to Albuquerque passed quickly as we raced down the highway and shared our story with our older brother Ken. It was a monumental moment, but a truly hilarious one too.

We did make it to the plane in time—just barely. We were the last ones to walk on the plane and they closed the door right behind us. I sat down in the seat and it hit me that I hadn't showered in the past three days. I had been working on a job all that day and was dirty and sweaty. I was still wearing the clothes I had worked in. But I didn't even care. I was on my way home to see my family. I'm guessing the person beside me was a little more concerned about my state than I was. I slept most of the flight home.

Brian

Our first job was a backyard lawn and putting green installation in Santa Fe. We could probably write a book just on this one install with stories like:

- The No Gravel Base
- The Obstacle Course
- Never use a Jumping Jack Tamper
- The Anaconda Roll
- Face Down in the Mud
- Distract Him, I'm Bleeding!
- I Think You Cut it the Wrong Way
- Who Needs Holes in a Putting Green Anyway

However, perhaps the story that has stuck with me the most didn't even happen on the job site. It was our second or third day into the job and we had prepared the base as much as we could and rough cut the area of the putting green. The putting green was laid out, but not secured anywhere and we had called it a day. That night we were back in our warehouse bedroom, and a wretched sound was keeping me awake. It was the sound of rain falling angry on a tin roof. When all else is silent, the sound is magnified even more. It echoed through that empty warehouse and through my head.

New Mexico doesn't get much rain, but when monsoon season hits, it can rain in buckets. This was my first real monsoon experience. It was perhaps the heaviest rain I had ever experienced. I laid there listening to the rain pounding down and I was more convinced with every passing minute that all of our work was going to be destroyed.

"Oh, that's it, our putting green is going to be washed away," I sat there in the dark just repeating to Dale.

I was convinced that there was no way our limited base and unsecured green could withstand a downpour this heavy. I fully expected to go up the next day with my tail between my legs and have to explain to the customer why his putting green had washed down the side of the mountain. Finally, Dale grew sick of my bellyaching and just said, "Shut up! What is the worst thing that could happen? If the green washed down the hill, we'll go get it and bring it back up."

I hadn't really thought of that. I guess that would be the worst-case scenario. I wouldn't say that cured my fears, but it went a long way toward helping me sleep that night.

The next day, when we walked onto the job site and found everything in the same place we left it, I realized how foolish I had been. I had given up faith in exchange for fear. The two don't coexist well, and I let irrational fears get the best of me. Even now, I sometimes think through this when I feel fear starting to get a grip. I think through the worst possible scenario and realize however bad it is, it will be all right. Most likely, my fear has no basis and is over exaggerated, but even at its worst, the One whom I have my faith in is far greater than any fear. There is no benefit to dwelling on what could go wrong. Rather I need to have faith that God has this all in His hands and whatever the situation presents, I can do all this through Him who gives me strength.

The truth is, this job was a series of unfortunate events. If the green had slid down the hill, we would have just climbed down the hill, pulled it back up, rinsed off the mud and fixed it. Fortunately, it was an unfounded fear, but even beyond that, the important thing wasn't just doing it right the first time, it was just doing it. Too often, we think we are chasing perfection by avoiding mistakes, when really we aren't chasing anything at all.

Brian

Despite all of our trials on this first project, the yard and putting green turned out great. We had a very satisfied customer and a beautiful reference point. Now our business finally felt real. If we could sell and install one project, we could sell and install one thousand.

In fact, looking back, I see this project was kind of a microcosm of our business launch and many other business startups. There is a dirty little secret about entrepreneurship that isn't often discussed. Entrepreneurship is messy. It's messy like my 4-year old daughter making her first peanut butter and jelly sandwich on her own—that kind of messy.

Sure, you have a vision and you start with a plan. You think you know what needs to be done. You've seen other people do it, but it just never goes exactly like you planned. We had wonderful spreadsheets and a well thought out business plan before we began. After a few years, our business plan looked fairly accurate, but for the first year or so, it looked like we were on a different planet.

Entrepreneurship is messy because it is inherently about something new and unknown. You can follow basic patterns, but you're going to bump into walls and have to adjust your path. You are going to have to live through some crashes and cleanup some messes along the way. I've read many books on how to start a business and how to be successful, but in reality, it never goes as planned because life doesn't follow a script. We need to learn and grow as we get messy and then we can get tidier as we go. The most successful entrepreneurs I've seen have learned to thrive in that initial messiness.

Not everyone likes it. Not everyone is willing to endure the messiness, but for those that do, it is a beautiful mess.

Brian

CHAPTER NINE

Show and Tell

Dale

That fall, we found out there was a product show that was coming up geared towards men. It was termed the Toys for Big Boys Show. There would be vendors there selling things like big screen TV's, games and game rooms, cars, motorcycles, and more. It was sponsored by a local rock radio station, and they were even having the Refrigerator Perry at the show giving autographs.

As I reflect on this now, I can see a disconnect here, but at that time, this seemed like a great idea. It was a chance to launch our product to thousands of people—people looking to spend money.

So Brian and I scrambled around to get ready for this show. We had no backdrop for the booth, no real signage, or anything else like that. We figured our best bet would be to put the grass on the floor of the booth and let the people experience it. That is what we did. Even though we didn't have the appropriate set up, it still looked good when we were done preparing the booth.

Brian and I had never done a home show or trade show before. We didn't truly know what to do or what to expect. However, based on what we were told, our customers would walk right on over to our booth and we would get business. So all we had to do was sit back and wait for the customers to come to us.

Well, the first sign that this might not be the event we hoped it would be was the slight trickle of people into the arena when the doors opened. That was problem number one.

Unfortunately, problem number two showed up right on the heels of the first. This was the reaction of the people to our product and to us. They laughed. I don't mean a humorous chuckle or an affable retort. I mean they pointed and laughed—at the grass and at us for being the ones selling it. They scoffed at us with comments like, "Look at that stuff. Can you imagine anyone putting that in a yard? That's a dumb idea. AstroTurf ? In my yard? Yeah right!"

It was a humbling event. Brian and I have a way to make fun out of any situation, so I can't say the event was a waste. We had our own chuckles and funny moments, but overall, we were hit with a back breaker.

Was the show a success? Judged by itself, no. However, we were in motion, we learned some things that didn't work, and we could now adjust and be better going forward. Maybe, more than anything, we increased our resolve. The more we heard that we couldn't do it, the more committed we became to making this business work.

Brian

Our first fall in Albuquerque, we had a sales rep trying to sell us advertising on the radio. She would stop in and offer airtime on several different radio stations, but we just didn't have the budget for that this early on. Besides, we weren't sure that radio was the right fit for introducing a market to synthetic grass. We felt it needed to be seen and touched. It had to be experienced.

One day our friendly radio sales rep stopped in and had a great idea on how we could promote our product. Her group of radio stations was running the Toys for Big Boys Show. We were excited and convinced this was really how we were going to introduce synthetic grass to Albuquerque.

Then the day of the show hit. Our radio friend stopped by the booth and asked what our promotion was. I guess our confused looks said with no uncertainty that we didn't know what she meant. She informed us that we needed to have some kind of give away; something to draw attention to our booth and help us get contact information from people on paper. Since we didn't really have much and we certainly didn't have any money to buy something to give away, we decided to enter contestants in a raffle to win an umbrella. We just happened to have a brand new umbrella that we must have brought from Ohio.

Now, I don't mean to offend any umbrella salesmen out there. Umbrellas are good useful things. However, let's be honest, umbrellas aren't the type of thing you'd expect to win, especially at a show like this, and especially in Albuquerque where we have 340 sunny days per year. Sometimes you roll with what you've got, and by golly at this point, this umbrella was literally all we had. Heck, our families were still 2,000 miles away in Ohio and we didn't even have homes yet.

Amazingly, that umbrella became a hit. I don't know if people in Albuquerque were amazed at this strange new contraption for this thing called rain, if they felt bad for us, or most likely just that people love free stuff and will sign up for any type of give away. Whatever the case, we got names—and lots of them. All kinds of people signed up for the great Albuquerque Umbrella Raffle. Yeah! Success. Well, kind of.

Unfortunately, at this event, in addition to finding a bunch of people that wanted a free umbrella, we also found quite a few people that didn't share our vision for artificial lawns. They didn't have a problem letting us know it either. We still walked out of the show with dozens of names and numbers on a paper from people who signed up for our raffle. We didn't necessarily call them right away. As the weeks passed, the leads got even colder. As we called, we found quite a few people that didn't even remember who we were, some that avoided a free estimate at all costs, and some that let us come out and measure

Brian

61

and give the proposal only because they felt bad. The one thing that we didn't find through this event was a customer. Zero. The Big Boys Show was a big flop.

Now, the truth is, I'm sure if we were to work that show again today, we would find some customers. Maybe we would find customers because our grass is so much better, maybe because we'd update our promotion, but most likely because we've gotten better. While this event didn't provide us any immediate business, it did serve a purpose. It was a great training ground. We learned how to set up for an event like this (and how not to). We learned how to engage with people. We learned to answer questions and handle rejections face to face. We learned to write up dozens of estimates, even if no one bought. We learned to hone our skills.

Unfortunately, people don't like rejection. I know I don't. People prefer to avoid the pain of rejection if given the choice. Pain just isn't comfortable, and we like our comfort. But nobody gets better by being comfortable. To quote a basketball coach I respect, "Repetition is the key to success. Do you want to be 100 reps good, or do you want to be 10,000 reps good? There is no substitute for repetitions." The Toys for Big Boys Show may have been a bust, but we got in some good repetitions.

Brian

Dale

During this time, although we had only sold one job and really didn't know what we were doing, we were already looking to expand to Tucson. Somehow, we had mentioned this to one of our software consulting customers, Randy, and he commented how he had always wanted to move to Tucson. At that time, he lived in Arkansas.

We talked to Randy about moving to Tucson and getting started in his own AstroLawn business. Our plan was to help him start in Tucson with training and support, and we would sell the grass to him for a small markup. This would enable us to make a little money and recoup our investment for getting him started while expanding our footprint and influence in the marketplace. We must have painted a pretty good picture, because he decided he wanted to do it. Anything can sound good on a phone call, but the reality of it can be something completely different, so we invited him out to help with our second install.

Our second sale was with Bic, the guy who was trying to figure out how we could put two pounds of rubber into one square inch. Bic and his wife lived in a beautiful home at high elevation, nestled at the base of the Sandia Mountains. We knew this would be a showcase job. However, it wasn't going to be an easy install. It was a decent sized yard and the layout was intimidating. There wasn't a straight line in the entire yard. It was all curves and arcs, and there were many rocks and trees to cut around. They even had a koi pond we had to work around. It would be fun, but challenging.

Having Randy out to help us on this project served many purposes and had several benefits. It gave him a chance to see the grass in the ground, which he hadn't seen before. It provided him hands-on installation training, which is more training than we had. It allowed him to meet and work with a customer. All of these things would help Randy get started in the Tucson market. In somewhat of a self-serving interest, it gave Brian and me an extra hand on installing this project. We completed the first job with just two of us, but that job also taught us extra help is good.

We were much more confident on this, our second job, but still had a lot to learn. It was a difficult install with the rocks, trees, and a koi pond. To add to the puzzle, in the middle of the desert in November, we got snow. Now we had to overcome the weather obstacle too.

As we laid out the grass and began to make cuts, Bic stood there watching us—another hawk-eye. I remember him telling Brian to be careful not to cut the grass short of the edge. I assured Bic that Brian knew what he was doing and wouldn't cut it short. I had barely finished talking when Brian laid the grass down and it was about eight inches short of the edge.

Bic retorted, "That looks like a bad cut!"

Much like at Charlie's, the big long rolls didn't fit or roll out so well in a small twisting backyard with lots of obstacles. While trying to roll one of the rolls out, and attempting to get the grass up over a rock and a shrub, we lost control of it and dropped it in the koi pond. Once again, Bic was watching the whole thing. He never said anything, but I think he knew we were not the seasoned professionals we wanted him to think we were. But we worked hard, were customer driven, and in the end, the job turned out well.

While Randy was there, he noticed that the brakes on our truck were sounding bad. We didn't have the money to take the truck into a shop, so Randy offered to help us fix the brakes ourselves. We went out to an auto parts store and bought all the supplies we would need for Randy to do a brake job. Unfortunately, once he started taking the brakes off, he hit a snag and wasn't able to complete the job. So, we opted to stick with what we had, and we set the supplies off to the side.

At the end of Randy's trip, we had a very satisfied customer, Randy was now trained, and he was making plans to head out to Tucson. So even though the brakes didn't work out, we were excited about where things were headed.

Brian

Belief attracts. Belief with activity attracts strongly. We may have still been quite green in this turf industry, but we weren't sitting still. We were making moves and taking chances, and more than that, we believed what we were doing was going to work, even before we saw results. This activity and belief became a source of attraction for both customers and team members. One of those new team members attracted was Randy, a customer from our software consulting business.

Early on, we knew we wanted this to be bigger than just us. I'm not sure exactly why or how, but we knew it would be more than just Dale and Brian, and more than just Albuquerque. So even with just one marginally successful installation under our belt, when Randy inquired about what we were doing, we responded in a way that painted a vision of what could be. While we certainly weren't recruiting Randy, we also weren't turning him away when he expressed interest in joining what we were doing.

As Randy showed interest and excitement, we told him how we thought Tucson would be a terrific market. Ironically (or providentially), Randy had been thinking of moving to Tucson. This seemed like a match made in heaven; we could help a friend get started in business and we could expand the reach of our new turf business. While we weren't sure exactly how it would work, we instinctively knew that if we could help Randy start a business in Tucson and help him become successful, it would benefit us as well. First step in the process, we had to show Randy the ways of a successful installation. With our second job on the horizon, we invited Randy to come visit us in Albuquerque and work with us on this project. Sure enough, Randy did work with us on the install and eventually moved to Tucson as well.

Looking back on it, I do wonder a little about what happened that week. I know we did a terrific install and ended up with a very satisfied customer. I also know there were some challenges along the way, like missing cuts in front of the customer, learning that it snowed in Albuquerque (who knew?), and learning that a power broom, rubber infill, and a koi pond aren't the best combination. What I can't remember are things like where we stayed and what we ate. This was still during the time that Dale and I were typically camping out in our warehouse and often feasting on chips and salsa or dry ramen noodles. Since Randy was a bear of a man (likely 6'8" and over 300 pounds), I doubt we had him sleep on the warehouse floor and dine on uncooked noodles, but then again, maybe we did. It likely didn't matter. I'm certain it wasn't the food or lodging that convinced him to join us. Instead, it was more likely the look in our eyes and the sense of where we were going. Everyone wants to be a part of something bigger than themselves and something that is progressing and growing. That is exactly what our crazy turf business offered.

Brian

CHAPTER TEN

Family, Faith, but No Plan B

Dale

We ran a few leads and kept busy over the next week or two, but our next big event was going home for Thanksgiving. Seeing our families after being gone for so long certainly gave us reasons to be thankful.

This was a very special trip for Brian, because he was moving his family to Albuquerque shortly thereafter. With the holidays and school, Lorie and I had determined it would be better for us to wait until after Christmas to move our family out. The time together that long weekend was great, but we couldn't just relax. Brian and I had to rent a moving truck for our trip back and spent much of the weekend packing things up and putting them on the truck.

Still, it was a joy to spend time with the kids, to hold Makenna on my lap, and to sit and talk with Derek and Kaylyn. There was food to enjoy and great fellowship with the rest of the family. I had many stories to tell, and of course, we were thankful for all the blessings God had given us.

Another thing I was thankful for that weekend was the news Lorie shared with me. She was pregnant. When she told me, I kind of went numb for a moment. How could this be? We hadn't planned on any more children. The timing was bad—I was still going to be away for another six weeks until my family moved to Albuquerque. But the moment of questioning passed and we celebrated the gift of life. This, for us, is the ultimate blessing.

After a great holiday and time together, it was time to hit the road. Brian drove his family out through Colorado. Although it was a little bit longer to take that route, it was much more scenic. I loaded up the Penske truck and started my solo drive out West again. It was a little different this time, as I knew that my family would be joining me. There was a lot less uncertainty about what we were heading into.

Probably the only thing slower and harder than driving a truck and trailer (like our first trip) across the United States is driving an old, rented, loaded down moving truck across the country. Another two days in a truck gave me plenty of time to think about how things were starting out and what we needed to focus on. There were many calls back and forth between Brian and me as we took our separate paths across the country.

Money was an issue. We didn't have enough of it. This made building the business difficult, and of course made living difficult as well. But we didn't let this stop us. We cut back on our lifestyle and sacrificed things many others wouldn't, to enable us to put money (and time) back into our business. We figured we could starve if need be, but our business couldn't. We discussed how the expansion into Tucson would work. Randy couldn't get out there until March or April, but we didn't want to wait and miss the season, so we decided we would do a home show there.

The Albuquerque market hadn't taken off as quickly as we had hoped, but we did have two good jobs under our belts, and a few more leads to follow up on. Certainly the questions of, "Did we make the right decision?" and, "Is this thing going to work?" kept coming up when we talked. We never dwelt on that. We would dismiss those questions and replace them with others, such as, "What do we need to do to follow through on our decision to do this?" and, "How much harder and/or smarter do we need to work to make the business work?"

Those simple little twists in how we would think about situations kept us moving forward. Maybe the biggest success secret we found (not necessarily on purpose) was the "Burn the Boats" mentality. We had to succeed. We had no Plan B. There was nothing for us to fall back on. We left our homeland. We put our homes up for sale. We were moving across the country. We had announced to our employer that we were not going to be working after the beginning of the New Year. We had no retreat, nowhere else to turn. We had burned our boats. Failure was not an option.

So, with that as our backdrop, we rolled back into Albuquerque for the second time. It almost felt like we were coming home—but not quite.

As we got back to business, we ran some more estimates in Albuquerque and were able to land our third paying customer, Joyce. She was a very nice woman who wanted some grass and a putting green. It wasn't a huge job, but provided enough money for us to get through December. Without a doubt, God always delivered. It seems like every time we were at the end of our resources, a way was provided for us to go on.

Aside from Joyce, December was pretty slow. We learned that between Thanksgiving and Christmas was just about the worst time possible to sell artificial grass to residential customers. Everyone is thinking Christmas and not many people are thinking about landscaping or improving their lawn.

Brian's family moved into the house they were renting in early December. What a relief. The "warehouse as a hotel" experiment was over, and I stayed with Brian and Angie until I went back home for Christmas.

I spent my spare time looking for a home to rent for my family. It wasn't an easy task. I was trying to find a home that would fit a family of five (soon to be six) and would allow us to keep our family dog. That is a trick in itself, but with a rental limit of $1,000/month, it seemed nearly impossible. The homes that were nice wouldn't allow the dog. The homes that allowed the dog weren't that nice. Most of the homes under our budget didn't look like the type of homes or areas we would want to live.

Additionally, I was hoping to find a place that would make the family glad they were in New Mexico and not regret it. We were coming from a large home in Ohio. It was 3,500 square feet on over two acres and it was situated on a private lake. How was I going to pull this off?

After several weeks, I finally realized that I wasn't. We knew we were going to be taking a step back; I was just trying to make it a small step. About one week before I was to return to Ohio for Christmas, I found a beautiful home. It had plenty of room and would accept the dog. There was a catch. It was $1,300/month rent. I struggled over what to do. I talked to Brian about it (since we had agreed to keep the rent we would pay under $1,000). He graciously said he thought it would be ok for me to get this and it would be good for my family. I called the man and told him I was taking the house. While I was still unsure we could swing that much money with a new business, it was a great relief to have that task completed.

Brian

It was great spending Thanksgiving in Ohio with our families, but this time was different. Angie and I were filled with excitement and adventure, but the realization that we were leaving our extended families and moving across the country left an odd tension to the family gatherings.

Since our home sold, Angie had been living with her parents, Steve and Susie. I know it was great for her, Julia, and Paige to have this time with them, but it also made the farewell even harder. Throughout this transition, Steve and Susie were awesome. I hope someday I can be that gracious with my son-in-law. I know it broke their hearts to see us go, but they never made it about themselves. It was always about us and they were always encouraging.

As we left, Angie's sisters were there to see us off as well. It was a tear filled sendoff as we started our westward trek. Julia and Paige weren't old enough to understand that we were moving away and that they wouldn't see their grandparents and aunts nearly as much any more. As we pulled out one of the girls asked Angie, "Why is Grandma crying?" While it wasn't easy, we knew it was right, and we were committed. This was the next step in our journey.

Unfortunately, we had two cars to drive, so Angie and I took turns driving with the kids or driving solo. Dale was returning to Albuquerque in a moving truck packed with belongings for both our families. I remember driving through the mountains of Colorado and the excitement I had just wanting to get to our new home. When we did pull into Albuquerque, the big surprise I had for my family was that I had our new rental home decorated with Christmas lights. I don't know when I had the time to do it, but it was important that it felt like home to Angie and the girls. After arriving and meeting Dale at our new home, the five of us decorated the Christmas tree even before unpacking all of the boxes. It was starting to feel like home after all. Lorie and the kids were coming out to join Dale over the Christmas season and then we'd all be New Mexicans, no more split families.

There was a lot going on personally, but we couldn't lose focus on what we needed to do to keep our business moving forward. We had to adjust to this new normal in our family lives quickly.

Brian

Dale

I love Christmas. Celebrating the birth of our Savior, time spent with family, Christmas trees and decorations all make it such a wonderful time. That Christmas was different. It was more exciting to see Lorie and the kids after not having seen them since Thanksgiving, but it was definitely different. I wasn't there for all the fun times leading up to Christmas and the move was hanging over us.

Yes, we were excited, but we were also scared. Lorie and the kids were leaving their home, grandparents, cousins, and friends. They were putting all that was familiar behind them and moving to a strange new land.

I know for them, the usually fun and relaxing holiday was overshadowed with thoughts of what the new home would be like. Time spent with extended family only served to remind us that we were moving and leaving them all behind.

We were leaving on December 29. We figured that would give us two days to get to Albuquerque and we could start our new life on the first day of the new year. It seemed fitting. We packed everything we could into the Suburban, three kids, a pregnant wife, a large dog, a hamster, all of our suitcases, and anything else that would fit. It seemed eerily familiar as I began to back the car out of the driveway. My family was with me and that made the event much easier. However, this was the last time I would be associated with that home. I grew up in this home. Lorie and I had bought if off my Mom a few years earlier. This home was the last thing of my Dad's that I had left. He had worked hard to buy it and provide for our family. He died back in 1987, and this seemed to be the one tangible thing I still had from him. Backing out of that driveway, again, was very difficult. As I shifted into drive, I stopped the car. I got out and stood in the road. I looked at the house, the yard, and I looked out over the lake. Was I ready to leave it all behind?

I was snapped back to the here and now by Lorie's voice, "Come on, Honey. It's ok. It's time for us to go." It is funny how she was going more into the unknown than I was, but she is the one that gave me the final push.

I am convinced the reason people don't have more success in life is that they aren't willing to take a step back in order to advance forward. They aren't willing to risk in order to gain. In this instance, we were willing to give up a comfortable life, a good paying job, a familiar home, and the closeness of family and friends. We were exchanging this for the unknown of a new land, a new way of life, a decrease in income, and a decrease in lifestyle. Yet this was also an opportunity to control our own destiny. (Before my pride gets in the way, let me state that God controls our destiny. However, He gives us gifts and opportunities to do great things, just like the story of the talents. It is then up to us to do this while staying in His will).

As we started driving, I listened to a new voice mail message that had come in earlier that day. Unfortunately, this message was from our new landlord-to-be. His voice mail brought bad news; he had rented the house to someone else.

What? How could that be? I had made it very clear we wanted the place over a week before, and he had agreed. My mind reeled. Here I am, leaving my home, driving my possessions and family across the country, and I had nowhere to take them. I didn't want to bring this to Lorie's attention just yet.

At our first stop, I stepped out of the car (away from Lorie) and called the landlord. He confirmed the home was rented. I asked about our agreement. He apologized, but said someone showed up in person with money, and he was afraid I wasn't going to show up and rent it. I wanted to challenge him on all of this, but what was the point. I wasn't going to undo what was already done.

I had to think (and act) quickly. I called Brian and explained the situation. I asked him to pick up a paper and see if he could find us some house leads. I told him if he had the opportunity, to set up a time for us to see the homes the first morning we were going to be in Albuquerque. He agreed, but he was under time constraints as he was taking his family to Tucson for the Tucson Home and Garden Show. I waited a while longer to break the news to Lorie. I didn't want to ruin the cross-country trip. Surprisingly, when I did finally tell her (probably somewhere around Missouri) she handled it incredibly well. She continued to be more of a blessing to this whole venture than she will ever know.

Considering we had a vehicle packed full of people and belongings, traveling across country was pretty uneventful. At our hotel stop in Oklahoma City, we did forget the hamster in the car for the night. The next morning, we thought it was dead from heat stroke. However, after getting it some fresh air and water, we were able to revive the hamster.

The kids enjoyed the country, the new sites, and the changes in the scenery. Crossing in to New Mexico was again, like crossing a threshold of a new home. When we arrived in Albuquerque, we went to Brian's, since we didn't have a home yet. The next morning Brian had set up an appointment for us to see a house.

The house was small—1,700 square feet with only three bedrooms and two baths, but considering our circumstance, it was perfect. We had found our new home. The catch to this home was that it didn't have a refrigerator and we hadn't brought one with us. So, with money at a premium, for the first six or eight weeks we were there, our refrigerator was a Coleman cooler in the garage. Again, Lorie took it in stride.

The Tucson Show was a big event for us. It was our first home show.

We were out of work and money. We hoped Tucson would help us change that. The fact that it was seven hours away didn't really faze us at this point. We just wanted jobs to do. It took all the money we had to get the booth space at the show and to get Brian and his family there to work it. Brian called me at the end of each day with an update of how things were going. It sounded promising. There was a lot of interest, and Brian was learning a lot working the show.

While he was there, my family was staying at his house—and we were defiling it. Somehow, the girls had caught a bug, and Lorie, Kaylyn, and Makenna spent New Year's Day throwing up (and throwing down if you understand what I mean). It wasn't a pretty site. Derek and I ended up watching Ohio State win the National Championship over Miami on a tiny screen in Brian's bedroom because we had set up a Mash Unit in the living room.

Within two days, all of the sickies were better and the new house was ready for us to move in. We were now officially in our new home. It didn't feel like home yet, but it did feel good. We were happy to have a place to put down our new roots.

Brian

While we had a couple jobs under our belts, the seasonality of our fledgling business caught us by surprise. First, it got cold in Albuquerque and it even snowed! Being from Ohio, we just didn't understand the effect altitude had on climate. At a mile high, Albuquerque was quite different from the Desert Southwest that we had experienced previously. Secondly, we could only sell lawns when people wanted to buy them, and sure enough, the holiday season is not a big season for landscaping no matter where you are. These issues, combined with some need for personal growth and development from Dale and me, left us in a tight position with cash and concerns for how we were going to provide "luxuries" like food and electricity to our families.

We decided our best option was to chase the sun so that as soon as the new year hit, we could get working and not have to battle the weather. While Phoenix was taken, Tucson was still a warm option and Randy had expressed interest in that market. This seemed like enough for us, so we registered for the Tucson Home Show starting January 2, 2003. Angie and I took our girls to Tucson while Dale and family stayed back in Albuquerque.

The Tucson Home Show blew my mind. An entire convention center was filled with items for your home like construction materials, furnishings, and landscaping. I had never seen anything like it. In reality, it wasn't unique, it was just new to me, but I liked the potential I saw. So much so, that I called Dale and let him know about the new world that I found. It was like a glimmer of the Promised Land. I had hope.

We setup our 10' x 10' booth by rolling out our grass, brooming it up, and hanging up a white vinyl banner that had AstroLawn Southwest printed on it. Now we were cooking. As I took my final lap around the arena preparing for the crowds to come in, something jumped out at me. It was another turf company. Now the amazing thing was this company wasn't just in a 10' x 10' booth with some grass rug on the floor. No, they had a massive display with rocks and pavers, lights, and the grass worked into the landscape like you might see in a backyard. What an idea! Then I saw their brochures! They were so professional and slick. I was in shock. I thought I was coming to stake a claim in a new land. I was going to introduce the citizens of Tucson to this incredible new concept of artificial lawns, and here was an established company who has apparently beaten us to the punch. My hope was dashed.

But hope is a funny thing. It tends to be resilient. It tends to defy common sense. It tends to look beyond just what is. As my father used to say, "Faith looks up. Hope looks out. Love

Brian

looks all around."

My hope quickly looked past this Goliath of an obstacle and looked out into a vision for our company. I mean, if they could do it, so could we. Why not us? We could even do it better! Armed with a new confidence, I walked back to my little booth and prepared to greet the crowds.

I don't remember a lot more about the show; it is a bit of a blur. I know that our friend Randy, who was considering joining us to head up the Tucson market, was there with us. I remember I talked to more people than I had ever talked with in a three-day period. I remember that Angie and I watched the Ohio State Buckeyes win a national championship one night that week from our hotel room, and I remember that we walked out of that show with a list of names. These weren't the phony "only in it for the umbrella" type names either. We had about 50 names of people who wanted to learn more about our offerings. We had hope once again.

Brian

CHAPTER ELEVEN

In the Arms of an Angel

Dale

Brian had a great experience at the home show in Tucson, but the experience when he came home was less than great. He came back to find that the Grand Am was gone. We had left it parked in a parking spot behind the McLeod Plaza. After we made some calls and prepared to call the police, we found out our landlord had it towed. He saw the out of town plates and thought someone had dumped a car there, so he had it towed and impounded. Brian and I went to pick the car up and found out that the bill to get it out of impound was almost $1,000. The car was probably only worth $2,000; more troubling than that was we didn't have $1,000 to pay.

It was another punch to our guts, but we had to keep moving. We somehow scraped together the money and got the car out of impound. We were very upset with our landlord but what could we do? On the bright side, he did give us a coupon for a free turkey as a Christmas gift.

Brian also came back from the Tucson show with a whole big list of leads. He assured me they were quality leads, at least more than what we got from the Toys for Big Boys Show.

So, we started calling. We knew nothing about Tucson or the layout of the city. We tried to look at maps to organize appointments by time and location, but we were only mildly successful at that. Nonetheless, after a week or two of follow up calls, we had more than a dozen people that wanted to meet with us and receive an estimate. This was amazing. The home show really worked.

In the Arms of an Angel

As we began to make plans for our return trip to Tucson, the realization that we couldn't afford to go there hit us. We literally did not have the money to pay for gas, food, and a hotel for us to go to Tucson and do the estimates.

Although we had no money, not going wasn't an option. We certainly were not going to call people we had appointments with and reschedule. We would lose business for sure. If we could get to Tucson, we could certainly sell two or three jobs, and that is money we needed. At the very least, we would sell one, and that would pay for the trip. We started thinking of ways to come up with money quickly.

After a few ideas that wouldn't work, we came across a winner. In the fall, we had bought brakes for Blue (our Ford F-350). That was when Randy was out for one of the installs, and he was going to put them on for us. Unfortunately, at the time, he was unable to get something he needed to work on the truck and he couldn't complete the brake job. We just continued to drive Blue with brakes in need of repair. However, now as we thought through this, we still had all of the brake hardware. A quick dash to the warehouse confirmed this, and even better, the receipt was still in the bag. We had found our funding for the Tucson trip.

Brian and I gathered up the brakes and headed for the autoparts store. As expected, they were great about the return, and suddenly we had almost $200 cash in our hands. That was all we needed to get to Tucson. Tucson was about 900 miles round trip from Albuquerque, so it would take us about $150 for gas, which would leave us a little for some food. We were very excited.

Brian

"Who needs brakes anyway?" Doesn't really sound like a sane question when you're getting ready to drive a truck six hours across two states, but since the choice was installing the brake parts or returning them to get the gas money needed to make the trip, it seemed like an easy choice. The truth is that sane questions and answers flew out the window when we decided to move across the country chasing this new venture.

We came back from the home show in Tucson and saw our first glimpse of opportunity. We took our list of potential customers from the home show and started calling through it setting up appointments. Now we needed to return and do about a dozen sales calls in one day, hoping to sell some projects.

It was still winter in Albuquerque and we didn't have many leads to chase in our new hometown yet. Tucson, on the other hand, had provided a much-needed spark. The truck needed new brakes, but that would have to wait. When the flame starts to flicker, you have to pour on the gas while you can. Pour we did. We returned the brakes, got the cash we needed, and made the long drive to Tucson squeaking and grinding all the way. We were praying not only that we'd be safe in our travels, but that we'd be successful selling some jobs. We were successful. We ended up selling five jobs out of that one trip.

Brian

Dale

To say the road between Albuquerque and Tucson is barren and lonely would be a gross understatement. There are stretches where you don't see any sign of life or civilization for nearly an hour. It is a beautiful trip, and you could easily mistake some of the area for a spot they could have filmed a lunar landing. However, to save on time and hotels, we made the trip at night. Instead of gazing at the beautiful shades of tans, reds, and oranges that painted the landscape, we stared at the yellow and white lines that lined the highways and back roads.

In the Arms of an Angel

We had been driving a while and stopped to switch drivers on the side of the road. As we got out of the car, I heard Brian say, "Look at that! That is amazing." As I looked over at him, I saw him staring up at the sky, so I turned and looked as well. I was amazed to see more stars in the sky than I had ever seen before. We were so far away from the lights of cities, buildings, and other cars that the light of the stars almost burst out of the sky. What an amazing sight.

We just sat there and simply gazed at the stars. How could anyone look at such wonders of creation and assign their origin to chance? I don't know, but at that moment, I gathered more affirmation of my beliefs and a sense of courage knowing that the Creator of all things had an interest in what Brian and I were doing on that trip. We rolled into Tucson just in time to clean up at a gas station restroom (we affectionately called this the Splash and Dash), and with little to no sleep, began our journey of attempting to do 12 appointments in one day.

We ran ourselves ragged all over Tucson. Not knowing the city so well, we would have one estimate on the northwest side, followed by one on the southeast side. Then we would go to the southwest and then to the north. We had to call and reschedule a few for later, and move others up, as we began to figure out where they were located. Nevertheless, in the end, I believe we made every appointment but one. They went well too. People liked the idea of grass. This was the first real large-scale acceptance we had seen to our ideas. It was a great feeling. It gave us the energy we needed to turn the truck to the northeast at the end of the long day and begin the seven-hour return journey back to Albuquerque.

Back in Albuquerque, Brian and I spent several days turning the crude drawings and measurements we had taken into diagrams that would tell us how much grass we needed and then into estimates for the work. We didn't really have a good system for following up. After all, we were seven hours away! We called some, mailed some, and emailed a few others. In the end, we sold five jobs and had a few others that we were pretty sure would hit later. Again, that was another "Wow" for us. In the first three months in Albuquerque, we had sold three jobs. Now, in one day of estimates we sold five jobs. It became obvious to us that the key to making this work was simply creating the opportunity to sell. In other words, finding ways to let people know what we do. Once they knew it, we could show the benefits of using artificial turf and make the sale.

Now the next challenge was to figure out how to install five jobs in Tucson. Where do we get the gravel? Where do we dump the sod we pull out? How do we handle rentals and such? Brian and I never got hung up on details; we knew we would figure those things out. The bigger question remained the same as from our last trip to Tucson. How would we afford to get there?

This time we would need more than $200. We would need money for a hotel, as well as money to buy the gravel and supplies to do the installs. We made it our practice to get 50% of the money at the time of the order, but with us being so far away, it wasn't practical for us to do this. We needed to pay for the grass prior to it shipping, and we couldn't do that. Somehow, Brian and I managed to get the grass to ship without paying first this time. I believe it was a mistake on the part of AstroLawn, but nonetheless, the grass was going to ship to Tucson.

Yet even with the grass on its way, we were still short money to pay for the trip and installation supplies. The install dates were set. We were going to install five jobs in one week. We didn't even know if this was possible, but we didn't think we could afford to be in Tucson longer than that.

The trip grew closer, but we still had no money. We were getting desperate. We had sold jobs waiting on us, but no ability to do them. I generally don't get too uptight about things, but this was bothering me. How could we get this done?

In the Arms of an Angel

We prayed about it. We asked God for an answer, some kind of solution. It seems that when things are tough, we always know where to turn. It is unfortunate we often wait until this point, the point of desperation. Nonetheless, that was where we were.

It was the day we were scheduled to leave. Although we had avoided it to this point, we finally began talking about calling the customers and delaying the jobs by a few weeks, in hopes we could find the money to do the work. We would likely lose some of the sales if we did this so it was our last resort, but we were at the end of our time. While we were sitting in our office preparing to pick up the phone to make the first call to cancel, the office phone rang. I answered it. There was a guy on the other end who introduced himself as Wes. He asked if we sold artificial grass.

"Yes, we do," I answered.

"Do you have any on hand? I mean available right now?" Wes asked.

"Well, actually we do," I replied. "How much are you looking for?"

"I need a 50' roll," Wes said.

My head started to spin. We had exactly a 50' roll in the warehouse. Could this really be happening? Who was this Wes, and how did he find us? That didn't really matter right now.

"Yes, we can get you a 50' roll. When do you need this by?" I asked.

"I need it today. How much is it?"

I gave Wes the price—I think it was $3,000. I had to also let him know that we didn't take credit cards.

"Do you take cash?" Wes asked, in an expectant tone.

"Well, yes we do. Where do you live and when do you need it delivered?" As I carried on this conversation, my mind was racing in disbelief.

Wes informed me that he would come pick it up. He asked where our office was and said he would be by in about an hour. Then he hung up the phone.

Brian heard my side of the conversation, so he kind of knew what had happened, but he wasn't sure.

"What was that?" Brian asked.

"I'm not sure, but I think we just got our money to go to Tucson," I said in a somewhat disbelieving tone.

Could this be the answer to our prayers? Brian wanted to know his name. Wes was all I knew. I had no last name. Brian wanted to know where he lived. I had no idea. Brian was curious what he was using it for. I didn't have a clue. All I knew was that his name was Wes, and he was about to pay $3,000 cash for the grass we had in our warehouse.

"At least tell me you got his phone number?" Brian pleaded.

Unfortunately, I didn't have it. So now we had to wait to find out if this was real. We called the girls to confirm that we would be going to Tucson, pending Wes' arrival. I was actually going to take my family on this trip. They had been in Albuquerque for a little over a month, and we still didn't have a refrigerator. Lorie was three months pregnant, and I had a bad feeling about leaving them for a week with no money and no refrigerator. I didn't think that would be too good for morale around the house. I was hoping to have a way to take them with us. I told her to start getting things ready for the trip.

The next hour or so seemed more like an eternity, as we waited for this unknown person to show up at our door. As the clock went past the hour, every minute beyond began to dampen our expectation. Was this guy real? Was he really going to show up and deliver us?

About an hour and a half or so after that call, a young man walked through the front door of our office. It was Wes, and he was carrying a bag of money. He counted out $3,000 and handed it to me. We then went around back and loaded the grass on his truck.

With that, Wes was gone and we had our money. We didn't know his last name, his phone number, address, or anything else about him. I don't even think we gave him a receipt. We just exchanged grass for cash and he was gone. Brian looked at me and exclaimed, "I think he was an Angel."

We loaded up our truck, closed up the office, and got ready to go to Tucson.

Brian

Some stories just don't make sense and perhaps they aren't supposed to. Looking back, I can't say for sure that Wes was literally an angel. I'm not even sure how that squares with my faith. However, I have no doubt that it was a divine appointment. God allowed us to get to a place that we couldn't find an answer on our own and then He provided.

I've heard it said that many people want to see a miracle, but most aren't willing to put themselves in a place where miracles can happen. Again, I don't want to over spiritualize this and say this customer was a miracle. It certainly doesn't compare to water turning to wine, the blind seeing, or lame walking. However, I'm a logical man, and I can tell you that in the tens of millions of square feet of turf we've sold since this event, I've never had another sale like it. This was a time when synthetic turf was pretty well unheard of in Albuquerque, and we have a customer call us out of the blue, come within two hours of the call, and pay cash for turf, all exactly when we needed it. That just isn't logical.

Fortunately, it didn't matter if it was logical, it just mattered that it happened. This wasn't the first time we had an extraordinary event get us where we needed to be or direct our path, and it certainly wouldn't be the last. Wes' purchase was exactly what we needed to get us to Tucson, and that trip to Tucson was exactly what we needed to move our business forward. One step at a time this business was being built and it wasn't just following our precise plan. We chased the business where we were being led. That didn't mean that we lacked planning or foresight, just that we weren't bound by it. We knew this was bigger than we were, and we were willing to walk by faith.

Brian

CHAPTER TWELVE

From Here to Tucson

Dale

The idea of taking my family seemed like a good one at first. It would get them out of the house, they would get to see a new part of the country, and we could spend time together. What looks good on paper doesn't always turn out that way.

First hitch in my plan; I hadn't really thought about the hotel rooms. We could only afford one room. We had Lorie, the three kids, Brian and me all staying in one standard, two-bed motel room. Probably not quite the getaway my wife had envisioned.

Secondly, we had no money. While Brian and I were out on the jobs working, Lorie and the kids weren't able to do anything other than drive around. I think I left her enough cash that she could get them all some lunch, but that was it.

Third, when trying to install five jobs in five days it means long work-days. We were up and out at the crack of dawn and didn't get back until about 7:00 p.m. These three things were not a recipe for happy family time together.

The work was hard. We had to prep the ground all by hand. The first job we hit was a putting green where we had to remove Bermuda grass. It was like a vine. Pulling it out was terrible. Then on top of that, we had to install a putting green that had to be cut around a natural stone border. That means many tough cuts on an unforgiving product.

We got the first job started, but not finished, and then jumped over and started the second. They were expecting us and we wanted to stay on schedule. We now had two jobs in process. On the second day, I dropped Brian off at the second job, and then went back to the first. To my horror, there were waves and ripples all over the putting green we had just put in. It was as though the green had just grown a couple inches and was too big for that area.

I went back to where Brian was working and filled him in on what I had found. We both returned to the putting green and spent a few hours trimming and correcting the install. Everything was new to us. We had never received any training. We had no one to call to ask questions or run ideas by. We were it, so we had to figure everything out ourselves.

Finally, we were able to finish the first job, and we both went back to the second. We were making good progress, but we felt like we were a little behind. That night at dinner as we talked about the work, Lorie offered to come out and help us on the jobs. We appreciated the offer, but weren't sure that was the best answer. On day three, we had Brian working on the second job by himself, and I got started on the third.

Brian was able to finish job two, and he then came and helped me with the ground prep on job three. Another long day and we were falling a little more behind. Three days were down, but we had only finished two jobs and were starting on the third. We decided it would be a good idea for Lorie to help us on day four. Brian and I started early and left the address for Lorie to join us once the kids were up and had their breakfast. By the time she made it to the job, we were laying out the grass. After a quick training, I put Derek, age 9, on some easy cutting and securing the perimeter with nails. Kaylyn, age 8, was on nail duty as well, and Makenna, age 4, just kind of hung out in the middle of the yard. Lorie, three months pregnant, took over the pouring of the 50-pound rubber bags and running the power broom. Meanwhile, Brian went on to start job number four. This was truly a team effort.

We hit something on that job that I think helped define the direction we would go with our business, and we didn't even realize it at the time. We were done laying the grass, had the seams together, most of the edges tacked, and were already on to top dressing the grass with the rubber infill. Somewhere in there, it started to rain. As it rained, we saw that the water was running off the roof (no gutters in Tucson) right onto the grass and it was pooling by the corner of the house.

Now we did not quote putting any drainage in the yard, nor did we discuss doing anything extra beyond just installing the turf. However, as we looked at this puddle, it just didn't seem right. We both thought if it had been our house, we would want the issue addressed. Brian was on site at this point. We both wanted to ignore it and move on. After all, it hardly ever rains in Tucson, maybe only about seven inches a year. The customer didn't have a basement, so it couldn't flood the house. We were verbalizing these rationalizations to each other. Still, we couldn't shake the notion that this needed to be fixed.

We decided to fix it. It was the right thing to do. Even though we were a day behind, even though we didn't have the time or money to spend on doing this, and even though it likely wouldn't be an issue, we had to treat it like it was our house. We wanted to be better than anyone else was.

So, we pulled up the grass, dug up the base, and created a "drywell" to pull the water away from that corner. We brought out the customer and explained to him what we were doing, just so he would know; then we put it all back together. It was dark when we were done. Lorie and the kids had already left. Brian and I went to the door to collect the check. As the gentleman was writing out the check, he kind of motioned us to step closer. As though he were telling us a secret, he handed us the check and he pulled two $100 bills out of his pocket.

"I saw how hard you guys worked on this job. I really appreciate all you did. Here is the check for the payment on the job, but I also have $100 for each of you. You don't even need to tell the boss about this, it is for you."

Brian and I both looked at each other, then back at the man. We told him thank you for the kind gesture, but he didn't need to do that. We were doing the job we were paid to do. With that, we thanked him and headed out the door.

We needed that $100 maybe more than one can imagine. Taking it wouldn't have been wrong, but we believed we were doing what we were supposed to do. The truly defining moment of that job was our decision to provide quality and to do work with integrity. We didn't have to fix that issue, as it wasn't our issue, and he likely would have never even known about it. Yet it was the right thing to do. That would become one of the driving forces over our business as we grew.

We now had three jobs completed and two to go. Unfortunately, my family was done. They were tired. This wasn't what they had planned for when coming to Tucson. Lorie made the decision to take the kids and head home. Brian and I managed to complete jobs four (which Brian had already started) and five the next day, and we headed home late at night.

We were tired or better yet, exhausted. We had installed five different jobs, totaling probably 3,000 square feet, in five days with two people. We did everything by hand, and ended up taking a trailer load of dirt back to Albuquerque because we couldn't make the last dump in Tucson. We worked from sun up to beyond sun down and ate one meal (dinner) each day. But we got it done. We did what we set out to do.

As we started the long journey back to Albuquerque at about 10:00 p.m. that night, the satisfaction of knowing what we had accomplished seemed to bump the exhaustion out of the way. There is something special about achieving a goal, and something exhilarating about hitting a difficult one. We had put it all out there, and we got it done. Add to that the fact that we had just done about $25,000 of business in five days, and we were pretty fired up.

That fired up feeling probably took us to about 1:00 a.m., but there is something about a long drive, on a dark road, late at night, that just tires you out. So we battled the last four hours or so back to Albuquerque, switching drivers multiple times. Much like the jobs we had just completed, we were able to battle through the trip and we arrived home safe and sound.

We came back wiser, we came back richer, and we came back with more belief. We knew this thing was going to work. Yes, it would be hard, but that is easy to beat. You just work harder than anybody else does. Working hard has never been an issue for me. That isn't necessarily anything special about me. I credit that to my Dad.

He was a special man who was without a doubt, the hardest working, most determined man I have ever known or met in my life. I started working for him when I was probably seven years old. He had rental houses we would paint and fix up. He always expected a lot. He would be disappointed if we didn't meet those expectations, but when we did what he expected, that little smile he gave was like a million bucks to me. I learned then to work to a higher standard, and that the reward wasn't necessarily the money, but more so, the pride you can take in a job well done.

Work is simply a matter of doing. Anyone can do it, it's just most people choose not to. They choose the easy route or the bare minimums. That isn't how I am wired, so I have a hard time understanding that. The belief that it would work, on the other hand, was something we needed. Fortunately, we came home from Tucson with a whole big dose of it.

Brian

Tucson will always hold a special place in my memory. It was the place where we almost moved. It was where our spreadsheets first calculated millions in sales. It was the first home show we ever did. It was our first road trip sales extravaganza, and perhaps most importantly, it provided the much-needed spark and flame that allowed us to survive our first winter in Albuquerque. Without the Tucson Home Show, and subsequent sales and installations, I don't know that we could have made it to February financially, or if we would have had the belief we needed to capitalize on the opportunities in Albuquerque once spring did hit.

Tucson is also home to one of the most impressive weeks of work that we've ever done. Two guys knocking out five jobs in five days is an impressive feat. The fact that we did it only having experience on a couple previous installs and being in a strange place six hours from home was just amazing. I remember working hard and putting in long days. It was one of the hardest weeks we have ever worked. Perhaps it was the adrenaline and excitement that we were actually accomplishing something or perhaps it was the determination that we needed to get the jobs done and get home, but either way, we accomplished more than we should have.

It was a huge milestone for our business. Not only did we gain technical experience and confidence in our installation abilities; we saw even better potential than our spreadsheets had told us was possible. Most importantly, we gained positive momentum on this trip to Tucson.

Momentum is an amazing thing. It works in either direction—growth or decline, and it is a powerful force. I've seen its power both ways and I've tried to create it and tried to stop it—neither is easy. Similar to the laws of physics, an object in motion tends to stay in motion until an outside force acts upon it. Business momentum works the same way. It is hard to create positive momentum, but once you do, it has a power to accelerate growth at exponential levels.

Sometimes you just need a win. Like a hitter in a slump, or a team on a losing streak, you need something positive to create a shift. We needed something to generate that momentum and the wins we had in Tucson did just that. This success was vital because it fed our beliefs and our business. We could take this profit and reinvest it back into generating more sales in Tucson and in Albuquerque. More importantly, with this recent success, our confidence had grown as well, and that made us more effective in both markets. We could feel the momentum building. We were starting to roll.

Brian

CHAPTER THIRTEEN

Solution Selling

Dale

The big news in our house after the Tucson trip was our ability to get a refrigerator. We still didn't have the money to buy one with cash, but Brian had a Home Depot card, so we went out and got a refrigerator for our house. Lorie was never so excited to have a basic refrigerator. It wasn't anything special, but for the past six weeks, she must have made at least a dozen trips every day out to the Coleman cooler in the garage. Indoor refrigeration was nice.

At work, Albuquerque was slow. We sold no jobs in January, so four months in and we had still only completed three jobs in our hometown. The Tucson installs were a good boost and kept us going, but we really needed to make things happen here in Albuquerque. With spring just around the corner, we were anticipating that our workload would change, and based off what we saw in Tucson, all we really needed was exposure.

Although we didn't have any real disposable money, we did make the decision in January to advertise in the New Mexico Marketplace. This was a local monthly paper that carried a combination of advertisements, feature articles on local businesses, and general interest topics. The main reason we chose this publication to advertise in was that it was relatively inexpensive, compared to other media, and we liked Bill, the guy trying to sell us the ad space. I think we paid about $750 a month for the ad, but that was assuming a full year commitment. This was a big stretch for us, but with the 12-month agreement, they would run a feature article on our business in one issue. Bill told us that the month that ad ran, we would get so much business we wouldn't know what to do. We gave it a shot.

Brian and I were blessed to have the understanding that we needed to put money into our business before we would ever get it out. We didn't have the money to put toward this advertisement. It was a commitment that totaled almost $10,000 a year. Nevertheless, we knew we had to invest in ourselves, even if we didn't have the money to do it. So, we sacrificed in other areas. We didn't have salaries, and we didn't take money out of the business, except the bare minimum we needed. We didn't have a lot of food in our homes, and we had no money for personal fun or recreation. We were counting on short-term discomfort in exchange for long-term rewards.

The first ad ran. Our phones didn't start ringing off the hook, but we did get a few calls. One was from a woman named Linda. She wanted to learn more. We went to Linda's house and spent probably a good 20 minutes or more just talking with her, first about the grass, but then about us, and how we came to Albuquerque. She was a nice lady who seemed genuinely interested in us. When we went out to the back yard, we saw about 500 square feet of natural grass, with at least 50 dead spots from where her dog was peeing on the grass. She had a problem. We had the answer.

We were starting to figure out this thing we termed "Solution Selling." We didn't have to convince Linda that she liked or needed artificial grass. No, what we needed to do was find out what her problem was, and then show her how she could solve it. In this case, it was having a green lawn without all the dead spots.

We measured the area, thanked her for her time, and told her we would get back to her with the amount. Shortly after mailing her the proposal, she called us back and placed the order. We had our first Albuquerque job for the new year—and it came off that ad.

Granted, it was only 550 square feet. But a job was a job and this one would represent a sale of almost $4,000. After installing that job, I can tell you we earned every penny of it. The yard had a natural crown to it; it was higher in the middle. We had told them that we would remove about three to four inches of soil, build the stone base, and then install the turf. Well, once we started removing the soil, Linda's husband appeared with a string line in hand and we soon found out he wanted it flat with no crown. This was an issue because it nearly doubled the amount of dirt that had to be removed.

We pushed back just a little but quickly realized this was important to him. So, wanting to satisfy the customer, we began digging. Brian and I easily pulled eight tons of dirt and sod out of that yard, maybe more. We did it all with shovels and wheelbarrows. That was all we had. To top it off, we did this in the rain, so the dirt was heavier and everything was messy. I thought we were going to break the trailer we had so much stuff piled on it. The back breaker for us was that after all the work and effort we put in to pulling that sod, dirt, and mud out of the yard and putting it up on the trailer, we had to drive across town to the dump and shovel it all back off.

When the job was done, we had an incredibly satisfied customer. What is that worth? In dollars, we didn't know. However, it was critical to establish a business where people were happy they spent their money with us. Without that, what was the purpose of being in business? We weren't looking to burn bridges. We wanted to leave a trail of happy customers.

Brian

As a startup business, it is important to be wise with your time and money. If you aren't careful, both can disappear quickly. However, entrepreneurs can't confuse being wise with these resources with being stingy. The answer to the question, "How much time and money do we need to invest in our business?" was simple; all we had of both. The key to being wise was making sure that we did our best to leverage these and get results, not just activity out of these investments.

One important way we invested money into our business was with advertising. While we had drawn up a business plan and had a budget to work from, we really didn't follow any particular road map. Instead, we decided that we would invest every extra penny we could back into our business. Some of this was in personnel and tools, but much of this reinvestment came in the form of advertising. In fact, I'm certain that we invested more in advertising that first year of business than Dale and I combined took as income. From home shows and magazines, to direct mail and a billboard, we reinvested as much as we could. Truthfully, only a small percentage of it was effective, but the secret was we didn't try to pick the winners before investing. We knew some would hit and some would miss, but if we weren't willing to take that chance, we'd never see any results.

Time is another precious commodity for an entrepreneur. Often this can lead to trying to finish jobs as quickly as possible. We struggled with this, especially early on when Dale and I were the ones handling most of the installations. However, we learned a lesson from our father about the importance of a satisfied customer, and we were always willing to invest the extra time and go the extra mile to ensure we exceeded the customer's expectations. Satisfying the customer wasn't our goal, wowing the customer was what we were targeting. Sometimes this meant that we had to spend more time on a project than it should have taken. Sometimes it meant we did more work than we had quoted and perhaps lost our profit margin on a particular job.

We just chose to never look at it that way. We always knew we priced the projects fairly, and if we had a job that required us to go above and beyond what was offered to ensure the customer was thrilled with the results, we would do it. While that one particular job may have cost us more money than we quoted, we never looked at it as a loss; it was just an investment. A customer that was thrilled with our work was worth whatever it cost, as it would lead to more opportunities.

Sometimes with new businesses, business owners look to see how they can maximize profit on every job and they miss the bigger picture. It's like they have an orange and want to squeeze all of the juice they can out of that orange. They spend all their time squeezing this orange, trying to get every last drop out of it, and miss the fact that they are standing under an entire tree filled with oranges.

We were fortunate that early on we saw that the opportunity tree was full of fruit. The best use of our time was climbing the tree and picking as much fruit (opportunity) as we could, not getting caught up on the absolute maximization of profit on any one particular job.

Brian

SEEING IS BELIEVING

Getting a Better Picture

Brian and Dale took this picture on their first trip to Albuquerque to show some of the opportunity for artificial turf. (Ch. 4)

Brian and Robert, from AstroLawn, on the first trip to Albuquerque in July of 2002. (Ch. 4)

Brian in Santa Fe, during their first trip to
Albuquerque, after meeting with the city departments. (Ch. 4)

Dale and Lorie during the girls' first trip
to New Mexico in October of 2002.

Brian and Angie on the girls' first trip
to Albuquerque in October of 2002.

A glimpse of "Middle Earth" where Dale and Brian lived,
showing the day bed dressed in its couch clothes. (Ch. 7)

The first install of artificial grass in Albuquerque. This
section in front of the office was also the first missed cut. (Ch. 7)

For the first official AstroLawn job, the brothers had to
spike all the seams when the carpet glue wouldn't work. (Ch. 8)

Seeing is Believing

The customer, Charlie, requested a putting green with
his order. Above is the putting green without cups. (Ch. 8)

The first completed
installation in New Mexico. (Ch. 8)

The second job in Albuquerque. This yard was owned by Bic, who had called about the fill per square inch. (Ch. 9)

Almost every cut in this yard was curved. It was a complicated job and difficult to work around the landscaping. (Ch. 9)

A before picture of the install for
Joyce, the third job in Albuquerque. (Ch. 10)

After picture of the job at Joyce's. Dale and
Brian remembered to install cups on this one. (Ch. 10)

Solution Selling became a realization on Linda's job in early 2003. Her issue was spots from the dog, the solution was turf. (Ch. 13)

Dale and Brian removed eight tons of sod and dirt from Linda's yard to ensure they had a happy customer. (Ch. 13)

Solution Selling often meant using design elements, in addition to turf, to meet customer's needs and budgets. (Ch. 13)

A display used in the
Albuquerque Home Show in 2003. (Ch. 14)

Ken, Brian, Nate, and Dale during Ken's week-
long visit to help with work in the spring of 2003. (Ch. 14)

Pulling up, Brian didn't think he had the right address
for this job. They wanted their backyard installed. (Ch. 15)

Before picture of the job where Brian needed a down payment
check to cover the health insurance re-activation costs. (Ch. 15)

After picture of the backyard shown above. It was two years later
when they scheduled a front yard install (bottom of 108). (Ch. 15)

Dale and Nate getting ready to
work during late spring of 2003. (Ch. 15)

The grass installed and traded for booth space
at the New Mexico State Fairground in Fall of 2003. (Ch.19)

Most of the crew from the Deming install.
At this point, the crew was already down by one. (Ch. 21)

It snowed on the turf overnight.
A frosty way to start. (Ch. 21)

The first completed field.
There were four infields to install total. (Ch. 21)

Big Blue,
Dale and Brian's truck.

CHAPTER FOURTEEN

We've Only Just Begun

Dale

We had a home show coming up at the end of February. This would be our first real home show in Albuquerque. After what Brian had seen and experienced at the Tucson show in January, we were excited to see what would happen in Albuquerque.

We still had some calls we were following up on in Tucson during this time. One of them was with a museum. As it was explained to us, every year the museum would build a house, mostly through donations. They would then show the house and have some parties and entertainment over a period of time before auctioning the house off. The proceeds from the auction went to the museum, and the benefit to the donors was great product promotion to a high-end clientele during the time leading up to the auction.

One of the people responsible for this event must have seen us at the home show and they wanted us to donate the backyard for the home. This sounded great from the exposure end, but how in the world could we donate 1,000 square feet of turf. If we sold that job, it would have been $8,000 of revenue. Instead, we would be out the cost of the turf, the materials, and the time and money spent installing it. I think we both wanted to say no, but the "what if " got us.

We were trying to set Tucson up for Randy to run. He would arrive in March. This would be a great way for us to prepare the market for him. If we wanted to make this market work, we needed to invest in it. So with that, we committed to doing the project. All we needed now was to figure out how to pay for the grass and get it there, and then how to get to Tucson to install 1,000 square feet of turf.

We manipulated some things and figured out a way to get the grass there. Now we had to install it. Brian and I realized we needed a third guy to get a job of this size done. At about this time, we were talking with our Mom and she mentioned that her new husband's son, Danny, was very interested in what we were doing. Danny recently graduated from college and had expressed an interest in learning more about the artificial grass business.

Bingo! What better way for Danny to learn about what we were doing than to spend a few days with us on an install. This was similar to what we did with Randy for Tucson. We called him up and made the offer. We would fly him out and back and put him up while he was here. In exchange, he would work with us on the Tucson install and help us work the Albuquerque Home Show. It sounded good to him. He was in.

Danny was set to arrive on Tuesday evening, and he would return the following Tuesday, so we had him for one week. We had it all planned and we were thrilled to have help with the install in Tucson as well as the Albuquerque show.

We picked him up from the airport at about 10:00 p.m. and continued right on to Tucson. Trying to capitalize on our time, Brian and I had also set up an estimate to do while there. The estimate was set for 7:30 in the morning. We rolled in to the east side of Tucson at about 4:00 a.m. At that hour, there was no sense getting a hotel, so we decided to just sit on the side of the road and sleep in the truck. I think we caught Danny off guard with that one.

I have found that it is easier to fall asleep in a truck when you are driving than it is to fall asleep when you have to spend the night in it. Sleeping was difficult and short, but we were able to get some done. We woke up early enough to allow us to "freshen" up in the bathroom of a local gas station, and then we headed off to the estimate.

After the estimate, Danny was thinking hotel, but we didn't have time for that; we headed straight to the job site. We got there, surveyed the area, and then got to work on this project. It was a beautiful house, and we were excited to get our grass in it. We worked a full day until well after dark then grabbed a bite to eat. It was 10:00 p.m. by the time we left the restaurant and started looking for a hotel. Unfortunately, the first several we looked at were booked. By the time we found a hotel that would take us, we were 30 minutes from the job and it was 11:30 p.m.

We slept fast and were back on the job early the next morning. We had to finish this day so we could head back to Albuquerque. It was Thursday and the Albuquerque Home Show started Friday. We still had to set everything up.

That Thursday was another long day on the job, but we finished. We jumped in the truck and started the all night drive. Driving the long dark road back to Albuquerque from Tucson was always tough. This time was no exception. By Friday morning, we could say we had slept one night in a bed since Monday night and had spent two days doing hard labor on the job site. The weekend would be just as busy.

Now we were off to the Home and Garden Show in Albuquerque. The set up was interesting with vendors scrambling to turn their little booth space into a nice presentable area where they could sell their wares. The doors to the public would be open at noon. We only had a few hours to get ready. We put a 10' by 10' piece of grass on the ground and then added some features like paver stones and flowers to make it look like a front yard. That was all we had. We didn't have a backdrop or anything, just the grass and faux landscaping, a table, and some literature (which we had made).

We had printed up 150 flyers at Kinkos before the show started. We had so much traffic at our booth that by the end of the day Friday; we were almost out of flyers. I stopped by Kinkos again Saturday morning and had some more printed up. This was expensive for us. Printing last minute flyers on glossy paper in small quantities cost some good money. The flyers were almost $1.00 per page, but we needed them. I arrived back at the Convention Center armed with another 300 flyers.

We were beat by Saturday night, but there was little rest for the weary. Sunday's show started up at 10:00 a.m. Sunday was a repeat of Saturday, which was good. We were so encouraged. Both Angie and Lorie brought the kids down to the show after church. They spent a little time at the booth, but they spent most of their time walking around and checking out the other vendors. It was neat having the kids there. They were one of the main reasons we were even doing all this. I know they didn't understand that, but it was so nice to have them at the show. Derek and Kaylyn were probably old enough to get a feel for what we were doing. This was important to me, because I wanted my family to be a part of this.

By Sunday evening, we were ready to be done. Although we knew we would regret it in the morning, we decided not to break down the booth that night. We had a job to start on Monday, our second Albuquerque job of the year. The customer was expecting us by about 9:00 a.m. Waiting would make Monday busy, but we were tired and wanted to celebrate the successful event by taking the girls and Danny out to eat. This was a rare treat. We didn't have money to eat out as a family, but this was a way for us to thank the girls for all the sacrifices they were making and to celebrate the success of our show.

Monday morning came way too early. We had to get back down to the fair grounds and break down our display. It would be another busy day. After getting the show stuff loaded in the truck, we dropped the grass, pavers, signs and such off at the office and headed out to start our job. This job was pretty large. It was over 800 square feet, and she had a yard full of sod. This meant a lot of work to strip it out and prepare the base.

The sod cutter cut the sod into strips and then we would roll the strips up and load them on the trailer. Each roll had to weigh between

60 and 100 pounds. They were heavy. It seemed like they would never end. When it did end, we had a pile of about 10 ton of gravel waiting to be shoveled and hauled in the wheelbarrow into the yard where we had just pulled the sod out.

By the end of the day, we were dirty, tired, and exhausted. The only thing standing between home and us was a trip to the dump. Unfortunately, the dump was 30 minutes in the wrong direction, and when we got there, we had to unload (by shovel) all the sod we had spent a large part of the day putting on the trailer. That is a tough end to a long day, but it is what we had to do.

I am sure we burned Danny out. That was a week of work and activity that I think few could endure. Danny was a real trooper, a great help, and he did an excellent job, but I think we pretty well scared him away from wanting to do what we did. A big difference here was that for us, this was our life. We did these things and didn't think about it. It was all what was needed to make our business work. To someone from the outside, it was work, and a lot of it.

As a business owner, the effort put in is not weighed in terms of that moment, or the next paycheck. Rather it is more like putting money in a retirement plan and looking at the bigger picture. The return comes later and there is much more of it. Plus, we are energized by the idea itself, not by the money from any one job. Each accomplishment gets us closer to the reality of the dream we are chasing. I think that is why it was easy for us (and most entrepreneurs) to do work and put forth effort others just can't imagine doing.

We now had two jobs done in Albuquerque in 2003. We had a home show under our belt. The Tucson market was started and we had our first real print advertising running. We felt the energy and were excited to see what was coming.

Brian

A dog in the hunt doesn't know it has fleas. It also really doesn't know how hard it is running. This business had to be successful. We had quit our previous jobs and left that life behind, so we had no choice. We made the decision once and didn't allow ourselves to negotiate how much we were willing to work at every new hurdle. We would do whatever it took and we would run hard.

From the very beginning of our business, we had visions of pulling in other people and helping them get started in business. We also saw opportunity all over, not just in New Mexico. We had begun our expansion into Tucson (actually selling more there than in Albuquerque at this point), and still had our eyes on Orlando, Florida. Our Mom lived there, it was a common vacation spot from Ohio, and we felt the growing city centered on theme parks and tourism was a perfect fit for synthetic grass. Enter our mother's stepson, Danny.

Danny was a computer programmer, but was young and active. We had worked with Danny in our consulting days when we pulled him in to help with web design on a project. Now he had shown an interest in our new venture so we figured we'd give him an inside look.

He could come to New Mexico, work with us for a few days, see if there was a fit, and perhaps help us expand into the Florida market. The deal was simple—if Danny flew out to Albuquerque, we'd give him food and shelter and let him work with us at no charge. Seemed fair—we pay for the flight and he gives us his free labor.

When Danny arrived, we picked him up from the airport with the truck loaded and ready to head to Tucson. We were driving down to give away an install at a show house that we hoped would bring us great exposure and new business. However, it wasn't bringing us cash; it was costing us money—so we had to keep our costs as bare bones as possible. Danny really had no idea what he was in for on this trip.

We arrived at the show house at dawn and worked past sunset. We had to work quickly as we had to be back in Albuquerque for a home show on Friday. At about 8:00 p.m. we left the job site and began looking for a hotel. Amazingly, everything in the area was sold out. We floated the idea of sleeping in the truck another night, but the look on Danny's face made it clear that wasn't a good idea. We drove around for about 90 minutes trying to find some hotel that had space and was in our price range-under $100 per night. We finally found a hotel that fit the bill on the other side of town at almost 11:00 p.m. It wasn't the type of place you'd want to take your family, but it worked for us.

The next day, we got up early and got back to work. This project was the largest we had done up to this point and took everything we had to get it completed in two days. As the sun was setting on our second day, we loaded up the truck having finished our job.

"Back to a hotel?" Danny asked.

"No, we are just going to drive through the night, no reason to burn daylight," I said. We did grab a bite to eat, we may have pulled over and dozed for a couple hours, but for most of the night, Dale and I just traded driving shifts while Danny tried sleeping in the back seat.

We arrived home Friday morning with just enough time to catch an hour or two of sleep and grab a shower. We had to get setup for the home show that started that night. After our success in the Tucson show, we hoped this might be the break we needed in Albuquerque. Danny spent a little more time at the house on Friday, but he was a trooper and was right there with us when the show started Friday night. We saw some traffic that evening, and felt like maybe this was going to work. This was definitely not the same crowd that heckled us at the Toys for Big Boys Show.

Saturday morning came and the show was on. Before we knew what hit us, we were overwhelmed. There were people all around us asking legitimate questions about our fake grass, "What's it made of? How long will it last? How do you install it?" There was genuine interest and a lot of it. I remember at one point as my throat was getting sore from talking, I looked up and realized that Dale, Danny, and I were all engaged in good conversations and taking contact information. Each of us had three or more people waiting in line to talk with us. We had been waiting for this turning point. Maybe Albuquerque was what we had hoped it would be and we didn't make a wrong choice after all.

Sunday we headed back to the home show with more of the same. It was definitely our most successful marketing event yet. We walked out of that weekend with over 100 qualified leads. The dam was breaking and the flood was starting.

As we left the show Sunday evening, Danny was asking about our plans for Monday. Tear down the show setup and then start a front yard install. I think Danny was shocked. It didn't strike us as strange at all, that's just what we did, but having someone from the outside injected into the middle of our madness, he couldn't believe that there wasn't a break somewhere in there.

Brian

Monday was a full day of manual labor as we removed sod and installed a gravel base with nothing more than hand tools. It was a long day of work.

Danny inquired on the plans before his 11:00 a.m. flight on Tuesday. "Easy—we can get a good three hours of installing in before we run you to the airport." I think this may have been the straw that broke the camel's back. Danny looked at us in amazement wondering if we had lost our minds. To us, it only seemed logical. We had gone straight from job sites to airplanes before, but he hadn't. He got up at dawn and came out working with us, but he did negotiate a return to the house and a shower before the ride to the airport.

Looking back on it now, I get it. We probably weren't the best hosts, and maybe even took advantage of Danny's free labor, but at the time, it was just a slice of life. Those all-night drives to and from Tucson and working dawn to dark everyday were our normal. Doing whatever we could at every moment to grow our business was normal. It was just different from other people's normal.

Danny never did move forward with synthetic lawns in Florida. He moved on and did quite well for himself in the computer world, but I think that initial shock was a little too much for his system.

We had other early visitors that helped as well. It seemed like there was enough intrigue to what we were doing that people wanted to visit and often help. On at least two different occasions, our brother Ken came to New Mexico and offered some insights and ideas, but he also offered some much needed labor.

On one trip in particular, Ken came and helped us on a backyard install, not exactly the ideal vacation. We had to remove

Brian

121

the sod, wheel in the gravel base, and then install the turf. We dropped Ken off at the site with a shovel and wheelbarrow and left to pick up the gravel and run a sales call.

What we hadn't thought about was Ken's desire to work hard and impress. We had told him to take the sod and dirt down 4 inches. When we returned to the job site, Ken showed us how much he had accomplished. He dug out all the sod for sure, but I guess he figured if 4" was good, then 8", or even 12" would be better. That was a lot of dirt moving with a shovel. Unfortunately, it was a little too much, as we would have to bring that area back up to grade.

My initial response was, "Whoa, Ken. What are you trying to do, dig your way to China? We just need to remove the grass." We ended up bringing some of that dirt back in and buying some extra gravel to fill in Ken's ditch.

In the end, we had another very satisfied customer, and we were very grateful for Ken's help. The business seemed to be gaining some momentum and it was always great to have our family and friends experience that first hand.

Brian

CHAPTER FIFTEEN

Here We Grow

Dale

Money continued to be tight although business was picking up. Soon we began to realize that we needed more help. We had the sense that we needed to build an organization and make the business about more than just us. Even though money was a consistent struggle, we hired Nate, a young man we knew from Ohio through our brother Ken. Our plan was for Nate to be an installer for us, a young gun so to speak. However, we were getting so over taxed; he ended up helping us with sales and estimates as well. So, our three man team fought our way through March, running from sales calls and estimates, to installations and follow-ups. We ended up doing nine jobs that month. We had to man the office when we could because we had a retail storefront, and we spent evenings working through email and writing up proposals.

We were getting busier but the bills weren't always getting paid. Our financial struggles continued. Utilities are easy enough to get turned back on, but one day we received a letter from the insurance company announcing that our health insurance had been canceled.

"What? That can't be! I have a pregnant wife," I remember exclaiming over the phone. "There has to be something we can do to reactivate the policy!"

Lorie was now almost six months pregnant, and if we didn't have insurance coverage, we were sunk. I was sunk. Lorie, as sweet as she was, would kill me.

The uncaring voice on the other end of the phone, in an amazingly condescending tone said, "Well sir, if only you would have paid your bill."

Yeah, I get it. But, I didn't pay the bill. That is the reason I'm calling you. "OK, but what can I do now to fix it?"

"Well sir, if you can hand deliver the money to our office by the end of the day, we can reinstate your policy."

I got off the phone and looked at Brian. We needed almost $1,500. We didn't have it.

Brian asked me, "Will they take a check?"

"Yes." The answer was yes. They would take a check. After all, who needs money when you have a check?

So with that, we devised a plan. The money had to be in Santa Fe before 4:00 p.m. It was already after noon. We figured that if we got them a check right before 4:00, they probably wouldn't take it to a bank that day. If they took it the next day, hopefully it wouldn't hit our bank for at least one more day.

I took off for Santa Fe, while Brian got to work at the office looking for money. Nate had gone back to Ohio for a short trip, but he called Brian and informed him that he received a call on an estimate he had done. They wanted to do the job. It was a big job too, at almost $9,000. Since he was out of town, he asked Brian if he could follow up to complete the sale and get the down payment.

Wow. God's timing is amazing. Brian called me to tell me what was up and that he was going to give me an update once he got to the customer's place. Brian was excited, but what he wasn't counting on was God's sense of humor—or his desire for a great story.

Brian pulled up to the house. It was an older looking house, but what was shocking was the landscaping. The grass/weeds in front of the house had to be 3' tall. The place looked completely unkempt. Brian checked the address to make sure he had the right house. Unfortunately, he did.

He walked up to the door and rang the bell. A very nice, older couple answered the door. They were likely in their 80's. Brian wondered if they were visiting their kids or something. In short order, he found out they were indeed the right people. They invited him into their home. They were some of the nicest people you would meet. But were they really going to pay almost $9,000 for artificial grass. This had to be a mistake.

Brian explained why he was there and handed them a copy of the agreement. He then stammered just a little and explained he would need a $4,500 check to get them on the schedule. This wasn't easy to do, as this was the largest monetary job we had sold to that point, and if you aren't used to it, asking for that kind of money is difficult.

Well, Brian got it out, and they gladly wrote him the check (Surprisingly, they were doing the backyard for their dog, not the front yard). With that, Brian started racing for the bank and he called me on the way.

God was good to us. He had provided for us over and over. Based on our belief that this was the direction God wanted us to go, we decided to hire a salesman, Eli, and a person to work in the office, Priscilla. By the beginning of May, seven months into this adventure, we had not just developed a business; rather we had started an organization. The two of us were doing a little bit of everything. We now had a full time salesman, Nate became our lead installer, and we had a couple other hourly workers that helped on installations. Priscilla was the voice and face of our business, answering the phones, setting up appointments, and helping to keep us organized.

There were seven of us in all, and this was just seven months in. Yet the money that was starting to flow from the jobs wasn't going into our pockets. We were still living below the poverty line. This money was being used to pay the organization we were creating, and to reinvest into the business in advertising dollars and such. We were working God's plan. I don't think we could take the credit for coming up with this on our own.

Brian

One morning, shortly after our first home show in Albuquerque, an older gentleman walked into our office and began talking with Dale and me.

"I saw you guys at the home show recently and it got me to thinking. I'm going to sell this stuff."

"Are you going to start a business?"

"No, I'm just a salesman. I sell."

"Oh, ok, who do you sell for?"

"You, I'm going to sell for you."

That was our introduction to Eli. Eli was a cantankerous old guy. Friendly enough, but he sure had a stubborn streak. He liked to talk, and he liked to sell. He decided he was going to sell for us. At this point, we couldn't hire him. We couldn't afford to. We weren't even making enough to support our own families. We tried to let Eli down easy, but he wasn't going away. He was sure this was what he was supposed to do, and he let us know it.

"Sorry Eli, we can't really pay you a salary at this point."

"No problem, I'll just take commission on what I sell. When

should I start?"

Over the next hour, we talked and found out quite a bit about Eli. The more we learned, the odder this relationship seemed. Eli was old enough to be our father; we were just getting started. He was a Jewish man who didn't believe in God; we were born-again Christians. He was a liberal; we were conservatives. He was single; we spent every non-working moment with our young families. Interestingly, none of that seemed to matter. Eli was certain that he was going to sell for us.

As Eli was leaving our initial meeting, he threw out one more off the wall comment.

"Oh, I've got a girl named Priscilla that you need to hire. She works with me now and is great on the phones. She'll pay for herself in no time."

Well how about that for odd. Not only did Eli convince us that we needed to hire him, he brought a friend along with him. Priscilla came in and we "interviewed" her a day or two later. We weren't sure exactly how we would work it out, but we decided to roll with it. We hired Priscilla too. Just like that, we were becoming an organization.

True to his word, Eli started selling. Often his measurements were off, or he underpriced jobs, but he sold and we found the value of growing our business beyond just what we could do. Just as importantly, we found having Priscilla man our office and phone gave us a home base and created a level of professionalism that we definitely needed. From answering phones, to making appointments for us, to helping keep us on track with where we needed to be, Priscilla did just as Eli said. She paid for herself in no time. In fact, today we often recommend that a receptionist/office manager is the first hire for one of our new dealers.

Brian

Eli had a lot of unique sayings. One he shared multiple times was this little gem, "My dad always said—you don't have to be profitable, you just have to have cash flow to keep a business going."

Honestly, I didn't like that saying very much—of course we needed to be profitable. However, looking back, I guess I didn't understand that statement very well either. Yes, a business has to be profitable to be viable long term, but there is a magic to motion. Having cash moving in and out and just barely getting by is far better than having no activity at all. There are times in business where we've had to do projects at no profit or even at a loss, but that cash flow from a negative job gave us the money we needed for a few days or weeks to get through that time. Sometimes, cash flow is king.

In hindsight, it's pretty clear our introduction to Eli was providential. At the time, we had no idea how our relationship would evolve over the next eight years, but we were off and running.

As our fledgling business began to grow, we started hiring install help. By now, we were in full swing of the springtime rush and we were getting busy. We had Eli and a few other part time sales people, but we really felt like Dale and I needed to spend less time installing and more time moving the business forward.

One night when Angie was talking to her parents on the phone, I threw out the idea of them moving to New Mexico. I explained that Steve, her Dad, could just work for us and lead our installations. He had given us some money to help us start this business and he was interested in what we were doing, but I really didn't expect the idea to get much of a response. As we began talking, I started getting excited about the idea. Steve had worked in a machine shop for the last 30 years, but that shop was in transition and Steve was going to be leaving. I figured that this was as good a time as any and began to press the idea a little. The next thing I knew, Steve was in his truck and driving to New Mexico to spend three months visiting and working with us.

You'd think we would have learned from our experiment with Danny, but we didn't. We threw Steve right into the fire. Thin air of a mile high altitude, 100-degree heat, and single digit humidity doesn't mix well with manual labor. Steve was understandably whooped. However, Steve is one of the toughest guys I know. He fought through likely heat exhaustion, dehydration, and altitude sickness that first week and before you knew it, we had ourselves a crew leader. Now, if the environment wasn't enough of a challenge, we gave Steve a little bit of a rag-tag crew. It wasn't easy, but he made it work.

Steve made a couple trips back and forth to Ohio, but that summer he coordinated and led our installs. Having Steve on the installation side of the business was a huge boost to our operation. He was able to manage the crew and this entire process, and now Dale and I could focus on moving the business forward. It was critical to us that our installations were high quality. Having Steve oversee them ensured that they were just that.

A sales team, install leader, a couple install crews, and an office manager. This organization was starting to take shape.

Brian

CHAPTER SIXTEEN

Brotherly Love

Dale

God's plan didn't stop with the development of our business structure in Albuquerque. No, He wanted us to expand and brought another opportunity to us. Somewhat out of nowhere, I received a call from Ty Allen. The last time I had talked to Ty was the previous summer when we were exploring the idea of artificial turf. I had known Ty since the 8th grade, and by the end of 9th, we were best friends.

As happens with time, the contact seems to fade, but the friendship never did. When he called in the summer of 2002, I found out that he was operating a carpet cleaning business. Wow! That was exciting. There I was, trying to muster the courage to start my own business and Ty was already doing that. We talked a little about the artificial turf idea, and he had mentioned that he had even looked into that. But we hadn't talked since.

This time, Ty was checking in to see how things were going. He had found out we were in Albuquerque, and he was flying to Denver for a job interview. He said he was considering getting out of his business and had a job opportunity in Denver with a salary of over $100,000. Ty always loved the mountains, and this opportunity was just what he was looking for.

"Hey, if I'm as close as Denver, I figure I might as well stop down and see you guys. Albuquerque isn't too far away."

We agreed. It would be great to see him again and spend some time together. More than that, though, Brian and I got to thinking.

Wouldn't it be great if we could get Ty to join us in this business? The obvious answer was yes, but how would we do that? We weren't even paying ourselves, how could we pay him? Plus, there were already two of us (families) in Albuquerque, we weren't sure there was room for three, so to speak. Maybe we could start another market, kind of like we did with Randy in Tucson.

Our minds started spinning. As the trip got closer, we floated a trial balloon at Ty. We told him that we wanted him to take a look at what we were doing. It was pretty exciting and was going well for us. Ty was obviously excited for us. He is such a good guy that he didn't say no, but he did let us know that he was pretty sure he was taking the job in Denver if they offered it to him.

Ty and his wife, Karen, came down to visit Albuquerque on their return from the job interview in Denver. After just a few minutes with Ty, I could sense his interest in what we were doing, even though he didn't want to say it. I think Karen, on the other hand, was longing for the security of a paycheck and the mountains of Denver.

We took them down and showed them the office and warehouse. They met Priscilla, Eli, and the rest of the crew. We went out on a job and let him watch what we did. We also took him to see some finished installs. That night we got together at Brian and Angie's house for dinner. While we were eating our pizza, we started talking numbers with Ty, and before we knew it, I had taken a paper plate, flipped it over, and started to draw out a simple Profit and Loss statement on the paper plate (it had pizza sauce on it).

Again, I could see Ty catching the vision. He started asking questions. Where would he do it? We suggested Orlando. That seemed to get both his and Karen's attention. When you are from the North, Orlando always sounds good.

Ty and Karen spent the night at Brian's house. That next morning,

Ty got up early and went jogging. His mind was racing. By the time I got back over to Brian's for breakfast, Ty was drawing pictures for me of how things could be structured and what this business could look like.

He was in. Brian and I knew it. He wouldn't admit it yet, but he knew it too. I even think Karen knew it, though she may have still been clinging to the hope of a job in the Rockies.

They left that day, but we knew they would be back. It was just a matter of when. The good Lord had provided someone to help us expand even further, to fulfill our vision of developing a business of impact and to grow our reach. He didn't do it with just anyone. He brought us the finest person, a man I respect as much as anyone I have ever known. He brought us a person of integrity and character, a Christian man, my best friend, Ty Allen. We couldn't have orchestrated that if we tried. God is truly amazing.

Anticipating that Ty would join us in the artificial turf business, we began working on Robert from AstroLawn. They had set up some more dealers and we wanted to stake our claim while we could. It took a month or so, but Robert finally relented and agreed that we could have Florida as part of our territory. I think Robert actually said Orlando, but we heard Florida.

We had a few more phone calls with Ty. He made the decision he wanted to join us in the world of artificial grass. Ty was going to be an AstroLawn Dealer.

With Ty coming on board, AstroLawn Southwest was poised to have full functioning business operations in Albuquerque, New Mexico; Tucson, Arizona; and Orlando, Florida. This was exciting.

Much like we had done almost one year ago, Ty was going to sell his home, get out of his current business, and move his family to a new and strange land. He had set the end of August as his starting date. He was excited, but scared. We knew the feeling.

Brian

Ty Allen is a brother. He has a different last name, and doesn't really look like a Karmie, but there is a bond with Ty that goes beyond a friendship. Ty was Dale's best friend in high school. They were inseparable, and I tried my best to tag along when I could. Ty is the type of guy everyone just enjoys being around. Distance and life changes separated Dale and Ty a little, but they remained close in spirit.

As we were starting our AstroLawn dealership, Dale and Ty began discussing the opportunity. Ty had his own carpet cleaning business in Indiana and also looked into synthetic putting greens. He offered a little advice, but it ended there. Fast forward one year, and we were in Albuquerque with our fledgling business and Ty and his wife Karen were coming to visit!

Ty and Karen drove in from Denver, so we set up to meet them at a restaurant in town. Steve and the crew were out with the truck, so I asked Nate if I could borrow his car. It was a ten-year-old BMW with high miles. It didn't even need a key to turn the ignition. We jumped in and we were off to meet Ty and Karen. Ironically, when we pulled in, all Ty saw was that we were driving a BMW. He didn't say anything at the time, but I found out later that when Ty saw the BMW – he figured it meant that we were doing quite well. Little did he know that it was a little past its prime and was borrowed from our 19-year old employee.

We were so proud to show them our little business. We were just finishing one of our very first projects over $10,000 so we took him to see it right away. Then we showed them our 2,000 square foot office/warehouse setup, and began telling them stories of our business adventure. As we got to talking, the concept of what we were doing sparked with Ty. At my house that night, we began talking about possibilities. We simply couldn't justify bringing Ty to Albuquerque (heck, we were barely paying ourselves), but the idea of working together was spinning.

As we talked, Dale grabbed a paper plate and a pen and started to draw out a business plan that looked more like a spider than a plan, but the ideas were growing. We still had interest in trying to make Orlando into a market—perhaps Ty could fit in there. Maybe we could partner with him like we were with Randy in Tucson and train him to start the Florida market.

So, Ty and Karen had options for themselves and their two daughters. They could end their existing bad business experience and take a six figure salaried position with the safety of a big company, or they could roll the dice and jump in the waters with two guys who had started a new business in New Mexico and who thought it just might work in Florida too. Sure, we had no real market data on Orlando, and together we didn't have the combined income that Ty alone was guaranteed in Denver, but we had something else. We had hope and freedom.

To some the decision between a large salary and a paper plate business plan seems absurd, and in truth, it probably is, but that is just at the surface. Ty saw something that the paper plate couldn't show—our belief and the freedom of owing a business verses working a job. Having owned a business, Ty understood the risk/reward nature of opportunity. Sure, there was no floor with this start up artificial grass, but Ty had no doubt he'd enjoy working with us, and he believed we were going to make it work. Above all, while the salaried position offered a safe choice, a guaranteed floor meant there was a ceiling too. We couldn't guarantee anything except opportunity and fun. We'd chase the opportunity together and God willing, we'd succeed together which would make the success even sweeter.

Ty left and over the next couple of weeks, we exchanged some spreadsheets and projections. After much thought and prayer, Ty decided to pass on the security of the job in Denver and join us in our artificial turf adventure. He would start Astro-Lawn Southeast in Orlando, Florida. As Ty began to operate business in Orlando, he followed a similar path preceding his family to their new home. The biggest difference was that instead of living between a warehouse and extended stay hotels, Ty lived in a retirement village with our Mom.

We were excited to have Ty on board with us, and excited to be part of starting a third synthetic turf market. Ironically, all three (Albuquerque, Tucson, and Orlando) started by moving people across the country into a new place to start a brand new business. Starting a new business is a challenge. Starting a new business in a new area where you know absolutely no one is a huge challenge. However, along with that challenge comes commitment. Just like with our move to Albuquerque, Ty wasn't sticking his toe in the water to test it, he was diving in the pool head first.

Brian

CHAPTER SEVENTEEN

Limitless

Dale

We were approaching summer and our business was really increasing. AstroLawn was growing too and we heard of dealers in California, Idaho, and even another one in New Mexico. We struggled with the idea of another New Mexico dealer, as we were told we had the whole state to ourselves. However, after thinking through it a bit, we realized we were getting so busy in Albuquerque that we were having trouble reaching outside of the city. Therefore, another dealer in the same state shouldn't really worry us.

AstroLawn had also announced their first dealer conference. This was due in large part to our prodding and cajoling over the previous months. We knew we felt like we were on an island and likely the other dealers did too. We told Robert how important it would be for the dealers to get to talk with each other and to get training and vision from AstroLawn.

This event was in Las Vegas, Nevada. Brian and I knew we were going, but decided to take our families too. We drove down to Tucson, met with Randy and his family, and we all drove up to Las Vegas.

I think it was a good decision to take our families. It allowed the girls to meet some of the other people doing what we were doing and gave them a chance to get a short vacation away from Albuquerque.

The conference gave us a great time of networking. We talked about the product, some sales ideas, shared installation tips and more. It was a good event that lasted one and a half days. When it was done, we took our families out to see some of the attractions. We walked the strip but it was hot, the walk was long, and Lorie was seven months pregnant. When we got back to the hotel, Lorie told me she was cramping and bleeding.

We debated whether to go to the hospital in Las Vegas or to head back to Albuquerque. It was almost a nine-hour trip from city to city, with very little in between. Although there was a risk in driving, we wanted to be back with Lorie's doctor at home. We turned a nine-hour trip into about seven hours, but it still seemed like it took forever.

Back home, we found out that the baby was ok but Lorie would have to be on limited activity and partial bed rest the remainder of the pregnancy. This was the end of May. Lorie wasn't due until August. This was going to be a long summer.

I had to do a lot more around the house, keeping it clean and taking care of the kids, while continuing to build the business. This wasn't easy. Lorie stretched her bed rest limitations as much as she could to take care of the kids while I was out. She was tough as nails. Together we worked our way through the summer.

The continued steady business was good for my mind. It felt like we were figuring this thing out. We still had so much we didn't know and we were learning every day, but things were working.

We were not timid about our advertising. We had done the home show in Tucson, we did the home show in Albuquerque, and we were running our ad in the New Mexico MarketPlace. We also had our Yellow Pages ad and some small local advertising initiatives. This was good, but we needed more.

We found a real, upscale, glossy, full color homes magazine called Su Casa. Running an ad was expensive, but the allure of full color and glossy print captured us. The hope of someone in a multi-million dollar home reading that magazine and buying our product reeled us in. We committed to a year's run in the magazine (it was a quarterly publication).

We made another bold move and got a billboard ad on Interstate 25, just south of the major I-40/I-25 interchange. This was a full sized billboard. The ad featured two sets of bare feet (those of an adult woman and a child) standing on our grass. It was a great looking spot and garnered some good attention.

By the middle of 2003, we had easily committed over $40,000 to advertising. We still didn't think we were doing enough. We evaluated things carefully and spent our money wisely knowing that some would pay off and some attempts wouldn't. It was important to our livelihood and by summer, some combination of the advertising dollars was paying off.

In June, the New Mexico Marketplace ran a feature story on our organization. It was a big break for us and when the article ran, the phone started ringing off the hook. We ran more sales calls and did more estimates than we probably had in any of the two or three previous months. Between installs, sales calls, and preparing proposals, we were literally running from sun up to sun down. We worked 13 and 14-hour days, and worked on the computers at night. On top of all that work, I was still trying to help out at home with a bed bound pregnant wife and three kids.

We were exhausted. We were worn down, but we had excitement. There was an energy brewing. It was like being at the ocean and watching a wave building. Better yet, like being in the ocean and feeling the wave building. When it hit, you knew it would carry you with it. That is exactly what happened too.

July was a month that took us over the hump, or what we had defined as the hump. We finally did the kind of volume we were expecting we could do. We completed 15 installations in the month, totaling over 9,000 square feet of turf with sales revenue around $70,000.

Limitless

Doing 15 installations including full ground preparation, base prep, and the installation of turf in one month with one crew was a daunting task. If we finished a job early enough in the afternoon, we would head to the next job to get it started. We were thankful for the business and were reminded what a godsend our office help, Priscilla, was to the organization.

Eli had negotiated Priscilla in as part of a deal to hire him, and we couldn't have made it through without her. She was regularly working with customers to accommodate our busy schedules and ensuring we were doing all the tasks that needed to be done.

Record sales, new revenue highs, a developing organization, and expansion to Florida; any one of these could have been the highlight of the summer, but there was an event that trumped them all. The biggest news of all for me in July was the wonderful birth of my little baby, JenniLee. Mom and baby did great. Jenna arrived on July 31, 2003, a few weeks early, but completely healthy. I was able to take Lorie to the hospital, be there for the birth, and spend the next day with them. What a wonderful time and event.

Brian

We had started to see some consistency in our Southwestern business and told Ty to follow our exact pattern. Send out some direct mail or targeted advertising and go do home estimates and sell jobs installing artificial lawns—simple. However, we were about to learn something new.

Orlando isn't Albuquerque. I know, that sounds like common sense, but the differences were bigger than we expected. First, grass grew pretty easily. Secondly, lawns were a bit bigger. Ty put out his initial advertising and had a great response in inquiries, but the sales just weren't hitting. We hadn't really learned enough to help prepare Ty. See, what we had done in New

Mexico without knowing it was find pain points or problems of customers and then explain how our product was the solution that they needed. Unfortunately, we assumed that the problems and solutions in Albuquerque would translate identically to Orlando, but they didn't.

However, we also learned several lessons through this process. First, high activity can cover a multitude of sins. Even if the plan isn't perfect, even if the actions aren't exactly right, there is no replacement for activity. Throw enough mud against the wall and something will stick. Here are a couple formulas that we discovered in this process:

GOOD PLAN + ACTION = SUCCESS
BAD PLAN + ACTION = CHANCE FOR SUCCESS
ANY PLAN + NO ACTION = FAILURE

Secondly, Ty's move to Florida re-enforced what we had learned in our move to New Mexico: sometimes you need to "burn the bridges." Just like we had no options except to make this work, Ty had put his family's fate on his ability to make this business work. Failure wasn't an option so he had to find a way to make it work.

When you really look at it, these two concepts are interrelated. When there aren't other options, your activity level is necessarily high. Yes, you learn as you go and adjust the plan along the way (which we did), but there is no option except to work like your life depends on it.

Too often, failure occurs when we don't realize this pattern. We think we need to have the entire plan perfected before we take action. That isn't reality. Reality is that action trumps everything. Sometimes only once you are in motion can you learn what you need to adjust your plan and get to the next level.

Brian

Ty did just that—he worked hard and long enough to make something work with our existing plan, and then we adjusted it as we learned from our new experiences.

After a few months and some limited success in the Florida market, I was in Orlando at a home show with Ty. Home shows are a neat experience. You meet all kinds of people and by this time in our turf careers, we were getting good at working them. This one was a little different though. There were a lot of people there and loads of different questions. There were also many business and commercial contacts too.

Then, it happened. Our big moment. The answer to our prayers. We met a contact from Walt Disney World and we were able to get a meeting with their Imagineering Department. Wow, this was it. The chance we had been waiting for. This was surely a sign from above.

Now for anyone only recently introduced to ForeverLawn or artificial turf, let me hit the "way back" button for you. This was 2003, we had one product, and to be honest, it wasn't that pretty, at least not by today's standards. However, we were sure this was the open door that we needed to create a break-through.

Ty and I prepared a sample of our one and only product and drove to Disney for our meeting. We talked about what we were going to say, how we were going to be a perfect fit, and we imagined installing our grass all over their parks. Here we are world, our time has come.

However, things don't always go as you hope. We went into our meeting with a boardroom full of people and we fell flat on our face. It wasn't quite as bad as the Toys for Big Boys show, but I'm sure there was some laughter. Sometimes the open door slams in your face and it hurts.

See, the timing wasn't right. We weren't ready. They weren't ready. Our product wasn't ready. We had more growing to do, but we likely wouldn't have grown to where we needed to be for a meeting like this to be successful unless we tried and failed, even if it was a painful experience.

I've heard the only way to fail is to never try, but I disagree. We've failed many times. I understand the sentiment and perhaps it is just a matter of wording. Perhaps the only way to guarantee failure is to never try would be more accurate. Unfortunately, I think the problem may be that we as a people have just tried to eliminate failure to the point we are afraid even to use the word. I don't really like it, but I'm not afraid to use it. We have definitely had moments of failure although we've just not stayed there. The key for us was just to learn from our failure and not let it keep us from trying again. In this case, the "No" we received from Disney was a terrific blessing; we just didn't know it yet.

As we had progressed through that first full year of business, we were living job to job and our vision of the future was limited by our present. We lived in a little bit of a state of tension. On paper (or spreadsheets), we saw what could be, and had the belief it could happen. However, the realities of our present left us wondering if we were really capable of more than where we were.

One way this tension was evident was in our mental glass ceilings. I don't know what causes it but I've experienced it and I've seen it in enough other businesses to know it is a reality. We created limits in our head of what was possible. At first, it was the limit of a $10,000 job. Who would or could possibly pay more than $10,000 for artificial grass? Sure enough,

Brian

142

whenever a project proposal would come up with that fifth digit, something changed. Occasionally, we'd end up acting like Chris Farley in *Tommy Boy* holding our little sale, loving it, petting it, and squeezing it until we suffocated it to death. Other times, it was more subtle such as losing eye contact, stammering a little, changing our wording or posture. People could sense our lack of confidence in the sizable job and then it wouldn't materialize.

Then, out of the blue, there was a crack in that glass ceiling. The first job over $10,000 sold and suddenly it wasn't such a big deal. What changed? It's as simple as belief. There was no difference in our ability to do the projects, no change in the value of our proposition, but project after project started to hit over $10,000, bringing us up to the next mental ceiling. In our case, after breaking the $10,000 barrier, we unconsciously set a limit at $25,000. We sat there for a while letting our own belief level keep us from landing any project over $25,000 and preventing many customers from enjoying a great solution for their needs. Then that glass ceiling was broke with a sale of over $25,000. We would subconsciously set another ceiling, but thankfully would continue to break through.

The mind is an amazing thing. We had to learn the hard way that its power could be as negative as it can be positive. Even unspoken, or unadmitted, we placed limits on ourselves for no legitimate reason other than our belief. Once we were able to build that belief, we were able to grow to the next level.

Brian

CHAPTER EIGHTEEN

Risk vs. Reward

Dale

It's a fair question. We just hadn't said it out loud. Finally, one of us asked it. If we are doing all this work, and bringing in money, why aren't we making any money personally? We were running a good business. It hadn't even been a year since we moved out to Albuquerque. We had sold over 60 jobs, had revenue for the year approaching a quarter of a million dollars, and Brian and I didn't have any money.

We were running hard. It wasn't so much executing a flawless plan, as it was modestly controlled mayhem. We figured if we ran hard enough, and worked long enough good things would happen. They were happening but it wasn't making it back to us yet.

Brian and I took turns having our utilities shut off. No, we didn't necessarily plan it that way, it's just when you don't pay the bill the utility company shuts it off. One month I'd take the money, and the next month he would. We only took money when we absolutely had to take it.

Not counting personal tragedy, there is not much worse for me than getting a call from my pregnant wife, telling me that the electricity was turned off. I got that call more than once in 2003. I would hang up the phone and ask Brian, "Any chance we have a couple hundred bucks? My electricity was just shut off." Somehow, we always were able to come up with it. Sometimes, the money was in the account and we just hadn't taken the time to get it out. Other times, it wasn't there, but within hours, someone would come walking in with a check from a new sale. God always provided.

I remember even having the office phones shut off. That was really bad. Even when you do finally pay the bill, they take their time turning it back on. This time, it was a few hours that seemed like an eternity.

As we sat there, trying to find our money, we realized we already knew the answer to our question. We didn't have cash on hand, because we were investing it. No, we weren't investing in the stock market, or in bonds or mutual funds. We weren't even putting our money in the bank. We were making a much smarter investment. We were investing in our business. We were taking the risk the bankers wouldn't take. We were putting our money in AstroLawn Southwest—investing in ourselves.

We invested in people. We invested in tools. We invested in inventory. We invested in advertising. We invested in marketing material. We invested in infrastructure.

Yes, it was only the first year, but while our utilities and phones were being shut off, and we were fighting to keep our insurance paid, we never once missed a payment to one of our employees, and always kept our vendors paid.

Keeping in line with this idea of reinvesting, we added Brian's father-in-law, Steve, to the team. Steve was a temporary add, but an important one. Steve came from Ohio out to Albuquerque and worked with us for several months that first summer. It worked out great that he showed up at a time that we really needed him. He filled the role of project manager/installation leader for us and allowed Brian and me to focus more on the other aspects of the business.

Steve also was incredibly kind in investing his money into buying us a dump trailer. This thing could revolutionize our lives. Instead of having to end each day by being at the dump, shoveling off the trailer what we had spent most of the day putting on it, we could get to the dump, hit a button, and unload the whole trailer in about 30 seconds with one person.

This new tool was a true joy. One day, coming back from a job, I had to take the truck around the corner from our office to get a little repair at the mechanics. I only had a few minutes to get there before they closed, so I dropped the dump trailer in the parking lot behind the warehouse and shot around the corner to the shop.

Twenty minutes later, I came back to find an empty parking lot. The trailer was gone. In a matter of those short 20 minutes, someone had hooked up and driven off with the trailer. I was sick. Steve had invested $5,000 of his own money to buy that thing for us. It was something we had wanted, but we just couldn't justify spending the money. Now, once we had it, it was gone in an instant.

I called Brian. He was sick too. We called the insurance company. For whatever reason, it wasn't covered. We called the cops. They pretty much told us we would likely not see it again. They said it was probably half way to Mexico by the time we had called them.

There is no happy ending to this part of the story, just some hard lessons learned. Due to the timing and nature of how this happened, Brian and I were convinced then (and still are today) that this was an inside job. One of our laborers must have tipped somebody off and they came and picked it up. We had our suspicions, but no way to tell for sure. After 30 brief days of bliss, it was back to breaking out the shovels and 45 minutes of hard work at that dump at the end of a day. No happy ending and no money to replace the trailer.

Randy was still working away in Tucson. He wasn't blowing the doors off it, but he was doing some steady work. He had probably done about $100,000 worth of work out there, but considering he didn't move out until March, that wasn't too bad. The plan had always been for us to resell the grass to him, to make money off what he was buying. However, we knew how hard it was to get started. We had just been through it. So, we just passed Randy's orders on to AstroLawn.

Risk vs. Reward

We didn't make any money off our Tucson market. Again, this was part of the reinvestment plan. At some point, we expected we would recoup this money in the future. For now, what was important was Randy surviving and succeeding in Tucson.

Yes, the business was making money. But we weren't in this just to make money; we were in it to build a business and be good stewards of what God had given us. Much like the story of the talents Jesus told in Matthew 25. We didn't want to be like the servant who, for fear of losing it, buried the money the Master had entrusted to him. This servant was condemned for being wicked and lazy. Rather we wanted to be like the servants who gained back more than they were given.

Brian

Dale and I have always looked at this business through binoculars rather than a microscope. We realized early that this type of long-term vision was needed, but also wasn't easy. We've never looked at this business and said, "What can we get out of this today?" Instead, we look at the horizon and focus on where we could go.

As that first full summer progressed, our business developed from two guys chasing greener grass to an organization of about 10 people. However, we had no credit line to call on, no more savings to tap into, and no more favors we could ask. We had to fund our business day to day. There were many days we turned to a prayer for business survival and it was always answered, but survival is not success.

We never really discussed it, but we had an unwritten rule that we never broke; if anyone goes unpaid, it is us. This may sound simple, but when you have to explain to your wife or family why the electricity is shut off, or why the cupboards are bare, it isn't easy. Still, we never missed an employee's pay, and were never late on a pay period. We had made a commitment and our integrity wasn't negotiable.

One Friday we had received several payments and had a positive balance in the bank. I was excited to get checks cut for our team and then take home some money to get our families much needed groceries and pay rent. However, after reviewing the commission reports and payroll, I quickly realized there wasn't going to be any money left over. Our families would have to wait.

It was painful, but our employees never knew about it. We understood that we were the ones who took the risk, not them. They had agreed to work for a paycheck. We were looking for more, but with that opportunity, we also assumed the risk that there was no guarantee. No ceilings meant no floors as well. If we wanted the rewards of being successful business owners, we needed to be willing to take the risk and deal with the struggles that precede success.

We didn't focus on the cost of these struggles. It really was just a matter of perspective. We didn't see this new business venture as a dairy cow that we would feed and tend as long as it provided us milk on a daily basis. It wasn't something that existed just to serve us. Instead, we viewed this new business as if through the eyes of a parent. We felt it was our responsibility to feed it, care for it, and invest into it – not for the immediate return, but rather for what it could become. In essence, this business was our child and we were excited to see what it could grow into in the future, not what we could get out of it today.

CHAPTER NINETEEN

Pay the Piper

Dale

September brought us back to earth. After a strong two months of the summer, September turned out to be our slowest month since February. Brian and I wondered if this was the seasonal slowdown hitting already. If so, that would be bad news, because March is a long way away from September.

We had continued new initiatives into September. At Eli's request, we rolled the dice on getting booth space at the New Mexico State Fair. I certainly wouldn't have considered that, but Eli was convinced we needed to do it.

The fee for the space was more than we really felt we could spend, so we told Eli to get creative. He did. Eli worked a deal with the people at the New Mexico State Fairgrounds where we would install about 3,000 square feet of turf in exchange for the booth space at the fair.

The value of the 3,000 square feet of turf was about $24,000, which was far more than the value of the booth space. However, we really didn't have the cash to pay it, and they would let us set up our booth right by the grass we put in, so we agreed to do the deal. We certainly hoped it would pay off.

One day, while sitting in the office getting ready to go to the fairgrounds to check on the area we had just installed, I got a letter in the mail. It was from an attorney. I have learned that it is hardly ever a good thing to get a letter from an attorney. I should have known what it was. I should have expected it. However, it still came as a shock, and was a real blow to my psyche.

The bank had started the foreclosure process on my house back in Ohio at Lake Tomahawk. Living in Albuquerque, we were able to consistently pay our rent. However, I had not been able to pay the extra house payment for the property back in Ohio. It was up for sale the whole time, but the housing market was down. I had borrowed money against the house to fund our move to Albuquerque, so I couldn't just sell it for any offer. I had to get enough to cover what I owed, and we didn't have any offers even close to that.

Living in New Mexico, we struggled to pay the utility bills. We went without a refrigerator for several weeks. We didn't eat out, and we had a steady diet of rice, beans, and pasta. How could I have paid for the house?

We had money in the business. Jobs were flowing. However, I couldn't rob the business to try to save the house. I tried working with the bank, but they wouldn't even talk to me or consider any offers. I had to pay all the back payments or they would take the house.

The easy answer would have been just to take the money from the business. After all, this was my Dad's house they were taking from me. It was his dream. He was now gone, and this was the one tangible thing I still had left from him. If I lost it, I felt like I would be letting him down. It would also be a great disappointment to my brothers and my mother. The lake was always a gathering point for our family. The home was so big and the property so nice, we would get together on weekends (when we lived in Ohio), just to spend time together. I was about to lose the gathering point. It was one thing to sell it, but to lose it to the bank, that was something completely different.

Still, the house was an object. This business was my future. I had to be willing to let go of something I held so dear; to take a hit in the eyes of those who knew me; to bear the shame of having my home foreclosed on in order to grow and build this business Brian and I were chasing. The decision wasn't easy. It hurt me to the core. I had to choose my business. As a result, over the next several months, I would lose the house.

Brian

One of our sayings our first few years in business was, "We're just following the breadcrumbs." What we meant by that was that it often felt like God was giving us just what we needed to get to the next day or the next week. We didn't know how or where the next pay would come from, but we knew God always provided. It was like He was laying down a trail of bread-crumbs that were leading us where we needed to go. These breadcrumbs were never enough to let us get comfortable or make the hunger go away, but it was always just enough to sustain us and move us forward.

It's interesting how our vision of "just enough" varies with our circumstances, but I can tell you, our "just enough" was lower than we had ever been. When we signed up for this adventure, we didn't expect that we'd battle utilities being shut off, bills going unpaid, or times when we literally couldn't buy groceries and had to live on rice and beans. If we had known the cost before we started, I don't know that we would have still pursued it. However, we also never drew a line and said, "No, I won't do that." We were all in. We had burned our bridges and knew that the only way out of this path we started was straight ahead, there was no turning back.

Sometimes, God needs to strip away more than we ever expect to get us to where we need to be. Not just where we need to be, but who we need to be. These experiences shape us, they define and reveal who we are, and they show us where we need to grow.

There were many times when it seemed like bills had finally caught up to us or the bank would call and let us know we were overdrawn, but just when it looked the darkest, a ray of light would come from an unexpected place. A customer we had given a proposal to a while back would show up with a check, or a payment for a completed job would come in just in time. We'd make a sale that we really weren't expecting. Time and time again, just when we were at the end of our rope, the answer would appear.

We had an idea of where we were headed but didn't know the path to get there. We had decided we'd do whatever it took as long as we felt we were still headed where God wanted us. Sometimes the only way to survive was to follow the breadcrumbs.

Brian

CHAPTER TWENTY

Integrity is the Heart of Character

Dale

When we came to Albuquerque a year earlier to get started in the turf business, there was already a company selling turf there. Over our first year, we had many opportunities to cross paths with that company. I would guess they did more business than we did, but I would also say they were unethical in how they operated their business.

We had stories over and over again from customers telling us things this other company would say and do. We were determined to take the high road. We weren't in this for short-term gain, but rather a long-term business. Getting caught up in the shenanigans this other company engaged in would only serve to lower us to their level.

I remember being invited to a meeting with the mayor of Albuquerque and the owner of this other turf company. The mayor wanted to determine if the city would offer rebates for people using artificial turf. In this meeting, he was trying to identify how many people actually would use turf for their yards.

The mayor turned to me and asked, "How many people do you service? I mean, how many jobs a year do you do?"

"We haven't completed a full year yet, but I believe we can install close to 100 jobs a year," was my reply.

The mayor nodded, and then turned to the owner of the other company and asked him the same question.

"Oh, we install about 3,000 jobs a year," was his reply.

That was a straight out lie. I know that. Common sense knows that. I have a thing I call the "Common Sense Test." It goes like this, if you hear something that seems hard to believe, run it through the common sense filter.

This man stated they performed 3,000 jobs a year. If a company works six days a week, every week, for an entire year, they have access to a little over 300 workdays, allowing for a holiday here or there (like Christmas, Thanksgiving, Independence Day, Memorial Day, etc.).

The average landscape job, for a work crew of three or four guys, would likely take two days to complete. But, for my common sense test, I even assumed it takes only one day to do every job.

Simple math then states that to do 3,000 jobs in a year, if divided by the number of workable days (300), one would have to install 10 jobs a day, every day, without exception for the entire year, including Saturdays.

Also, to accomplish that, there would have to be 10 completely separate installation teams of three to four guys, out there doing this every day.

This story by the other guy didn't just fail the Common Sense Test, it obliterated it. Still, the mayor sat there nodding his head in agreement and seemed quite impressed. I could have blown this thing up right in front of the mayor, but that wasn't the purpose of the meeting, and I didn't want to stoop to their level.

I believe that, in the end, right wins and if by some chance it doesn't, my integrity is more valuable than any amount of money or looking good in the eyes of others (in this case, the mayor).

Interestingly enough, at our office, we would have a steady stream of people stop in asking for work. These weren't just people off the street, they were people who either had worked for the other company, or were still working for the other company.

We had all types; salespeople, installers, office workers, and project managers. It was like a revolving door of people fleeing the other company. For the most part, we just thanked them, took their resume, and put it in a file. The file had to have 25 or 30 resumes in it. On a rare occasion, depending on our need, we would hire one of them.

In October, Richard came through our door. He was the lead project manager for the other company. He said he'd had enough at the other place and wanted to work for us. We thanked him for coming in, but let him know that we weren't looking to hire that position and couldn't afford him even if we were.

He asked us to make him an offer. We didn't. Richard called back a few more times. He was persistent. He also got to know Eli; Eli wanted us to bring Richard on as well. Finally, we agreed to meet again and discuss the options. While we weren't looking, and we couldn't afford it, the idea of having a Project Manager/Installation Leader was appealing. This would free Brian and me up to focus on other areas of the business.

With the addition of Richard, we had a good December and decided we could take some time with our families and head back home to Ohio for Christmas. This would be our first time back as a family since leaving almost a year earlier.

We had one big job that had to be done in December. The job was a 3,000 square foot installation at Villa Del Este apartments. This was a commercial job and the biggest job we had to date. We went over the job with Richard and the workers. We explained the importance of getting it done, getting it done right, and getting it done on time.

With that, we boarded a plane back to Ohio the day they were supposed to start the install. As I looked out the plane window, I saw snow all over the ground and wondered how they would be able to work in those conditions and get the job done.

About four days into our trip, we got a call from the guys. It seems someone had stolen our blower. They didn't know what happened to it, but it was there one day and gone the next. They then told us they suspected that the maintenance guy for the apartments may have accidentally confused it with his stuff and put it away.

We weren't happy about the call, but figured we'd dig into it a bit. We called the apartment complex and got the head of maintenance that we were doing the work for. We explained that we were looking for our blower and wondered if he maybe accidentally picked it up. He was somewhat skeptical as he explained to us that he opened up his tool shed for them one day so they could stay warm from the snow. Later, much to his dismay, he found out that his weed whacker was missing and he was getting ready to call us to let us know.

My blood was boiling and my head was ready to explode. How could this happen? We were a business of honesty. Integrity. Now we were being accused of stealing something? We could work months, or even years to establish a reputation that could be wiped out in an instant. This wasn't acceptable.

We called the guys and talked to them. We challenged them point blank. No one knew anything. We called Richard, our project manager. He informed us that he got the guys started on the job, but they were doing well so he left them there. He had no idea what was going on. I was tempted to get on a plane and fly out there and interrogate each one of them, but common sense got the better of me.

As Brian and I started to recount the last few months, several tools had come up missing. Little things like drills, saws, knives, and other small tools. Nothing big was taken, other than the dump trailer. At the time, we had chalked this up to things being lost or forgotten on a job, but now it seemed like we were seeing a pattern.

We told the guys to finish the work on hand and that we would be back after the new year. Then, not more than a day or two later, we received a call from one of the guys telling us they were on a job site and had locked the keys in the truck. There was some convoluted story about them seeing someone they thought was going to steal some stuff while they were on the job, so they locked the doors to the truck and the keys were in it. Along with that, they claimed another tool was stolen while they were working on the job. Just the way the whole thing went down, that was the last straw. Maybe it wasn't smart, but right then, over the phone, we fired all of them. We told them to pack up the stuff, get it back to the warehouse, and turn in all their tools. We would pay them what we owed them and that was it. They were done. Merry Christmas.

We finished December by flying down to Florida and working with Ty on a 7,500 square foot playground. This was bigger than any job we had ever seen. It was quite an experience, and again, a real confidence builder. Seeing something of this size and in a new arena for us—playgrounds—opened up a completely new realm of what was possible.

Looking back at our first full calendar year, we were quite amazed with how blessed we were and at what we were able to accomplish. We sold/installed about 55,000 square feet of turf. This equated to almost a half million-dollar business. Considering we were in a new land, knowing no one, and selling a product we were really never trained or taught on, we were pretty happy with how things were going.

In addition to what was happening in Albuquerque, we had our market in Tucson where we (and Randy) had probably sold/installed another 20,000 square feet, and Ty was now rolling in Florida. This was exciting. One year earlier, we had only done three jobs leading into the year and had nothing on the horizon. We got very excited thinking about what the year 2004 would have in store for us. We were now established; we understood the product and the business much better. The sky was the limit.

Brian

We called it the grocery store test. Kind of a silly name, but Dale and I both knew our name and our integrity was critical to long-term success. We discussed a fictional scenario where we ran into a customer of ours in a grocery store a few years after we had done their project and asked ourselves, "How would they respond?" Would we be excited to see them and ask about their yard, and would they be happy to see us and still be pleased with our work? Ironically, this fictional fast-forward played out in reality more than once, and it even happened in an actual grocery store. Fortunately, the results were always great. Every time this happened, we met a happy customer and had a pleasant conversation. Even before we had these grocery store verifications, we knew we'd rather fail than exchange our integrity for short-term success.

Our first full calendar year in business was a successful one. First of all, we had survived. More than that, we had grown into a structure that allowed our business to do work and earn income even when we weren't there. This wasn't easy. It required reinvesting every penny we could back into our business, but we knew this investment in expanding our team would pay off both in the long run in our profitability, and in the short term by giving us some glimpses of freedom. Christmas time seemed like a great time to test this out, so we did. Dale and I both traveled back to Ohio with our families over Christmas and left our crew to complete a large commercial project in Albuquerque.

Integrity is the Heart of Character

Real life is never as smooth as your plans. Unfortunately, our Christmas vacation was interrupted by calls from Albuquerque about missing items and potential theft on the job-site. The guys we had working were young, rough, and apparently needed more supervision than they were being given. However, after some questioning, it became clear that we had both thieves and liars working for us. This just wasn't acceptable. We couldn't afford to have a crew that would bring our integrity into question. A good reputation takes a lifetime to build and just a moment to destroy. Since no one on our team was willing to come clean about what was going on, we had to let them all go.

Firing someone is never easy. Firing someone at Christmas is even harder. Doing it from 2,000 miles away probably isn't smart. However, sometimes you just have to play the hand you are dealt. I am sure that when the guys on the crew returned the truck, trailer, and tools to the office, we lost quite a few more items. I'm really not sure how much money we lost on these stolen items or the cost of hiring and retraining a new crew, but I am certain it was far less than the value of our integrity and trust.

That Christmas break wasn't all bad. Although we had our challenges in Albuquerque, Ty was finding success in Florida.

"How big did you say? 7,500 square feet? In one project?" I asked Ty.

That was the start of a conversation with Ty in December of 2003. Ty had plodded along in Florida selling jobs here and there, but hadn't hit full stride yet, that was about to change. Ty came across an opportunity to install artificial grass in a playground at a private school in South Florida. It was the largest single job either of us had sold. This sale would more than double our largest up to that date.

Ty (in great Karmie-like form) sold the project and then realized he needed to figure out how to get it installed. Of course, he gave Dale and me a call to see if we were up to help with the challenge. Between Christmas and New Year's seemed like the perfect time for a trip to Florida for an install, and that's exactly what we did.

Dale and I took a break from our Christmas vacation in Ohio and flew down to join Ty and his father-in-law, Tony, on the largest installation we had seen up to that point. I remember walking onto the job site and thinking, "Are you kidding me? The four of us are going to install all of this turf in just four days? Is that even possible?" By the grace of God, and with the help of adrenaline, we got it done. We worked nonstop, dawn to dark, every day.

We didn't have much money for eating out, so Ty was kind enough to grab a loaf of bread and jar of peanut butter for our lunches. I doubt we even had jelly, but that was ok because just being a part of this project was a joy and built our belief. I mean someone liked our product enough to invest over $50,000 in one playground area. This was going to work. Even in Florida.

Brian

CHAPTER TWENTY-ONE

The Deming Debacle

Dale

Welcome 2004. Now, to add to the excitement of finishing our first full year, we received a call from someone at Southwest Recreational Industries (SRI) in early January. This was the parent company to AstroLawn and they also owned a sports field division. Over the past 16 months, we had been pestering people at SRI, asking them to let us be involved in a sports field installation. They didn't even have to pay us, if they would just invite us on a job so we could learn. We really wanted to become involved in selling and installing sports fields.

The call was more than we could have expected. They had four baseball infields they had sold in Deming, New Mexico. However, they weren't calling to ask us if we could come down and work with them to learn it; they were asking us to give them a bid to install these four fields! Wow. I couldn't believe it. We had never been involved in a field installation of any type. The closest we got to one was back in 2002 (before we had even started as dealers), when Brian went down to the field at Mount Union College and watched for a few hours as they put in the field. It didn't quite qualify as certification.

Well, as has always been our way, we told SRI that we could do it and would like to do it. Now we had to get them a quote. We came up with a number of $40,000. This was to install the turf and included the supplies. They accepted.

Just like that, we were in the sports field business. The catch for us was that we needed about $15,000 to buy the supplies to do the job, and we wouldn't be paid until it was done. We had a little money, but not much. Although our previous year was good, we put all of the money back into advertising, promotion, tools and supplies, personnel, and expansion to Tucson and Florida.

Not having the money to purchase the supplies, we called our brother Ken. We explained the situation to him. We told him we needed about $10,000 to buy the things we needed, and we would be paying him back as soon as we got the $40,000 from SRI, which should be within 30 days of completing the project. We would borrow $10,000 and pay back $12,000. It was a pretty straightforward move and Ken was a big supporter of us, so he agreed. He pulled the money out of one of his investments and sent it over. We were ready to roll.

Now that the money was taken care of, we needed to assemble a crew since we no longer had one. We called Rueben, a guy who had worked with us before. He agreed to come. We also called and invited Steve, a concrete curb installation guy, whose concrete curbs we used on many of our jobs. Steve had never worked with us on actually installing turf before.

We then called Randy in Tucson and told him we had a chance for him and his guys to earn some money and work on a field. He was in and would bring two guys. Now our crew was set. We had seven people descending on Deming in the beginning of February 2004. We didn't quite know what we were getting ourselves into, but we were sure we could figure it out.

God has a purpose for everything. I don't question that. However, I often wonder what the purpose is. We arrived in Deming to the coldest spell they had in recent years. The temperatures in the morning were in the teens, and by afternoon, it would eventually warm up into the 20's. There was snow. It was cold and we were unprepared for that.

In addition to the elements, the rolls of grass were large and the project somewhat daunting. The first day, we got a feel for the job and what we were up against. We even got several rolls of turf rolled out and in place. It looked like things were going to work out. That night it got even colder and in the morning, snow covered the fields and the grass we had already rolled out. We spent the first hour of the day using shovels and brooms to clean the snow off the fields so we could work on seams and continue installing more turf.

Then the problems started. First, it was Steve. After the first full day on the job (and dealing with cold weather), Steve received a "phone call" from back home, and he said he needed to go. It was unfortunate since we needed the manpower, but what could we do. On day two, the remaining six of us worked long and hard and accomplished some good things. Then, on the morning of day three, we took another blow. As we met in the hotel lobby in the morning to head out to the job, we noticed that Randy and his guys had their luggage with them. Randy informed us they had something "come up" and they needed to be back in Tucson by the end of the day. They would work day three but then they were going to be gone. Seriously? Here we sat on the largest project we had ever done, the first fields we had ever done, and we had three guys to finish the job; Brian, Rueben, and me. This was not good.

I had questioned God's plan a little when we got to Deming and found out how cold it was. Now, the cold was nothing compared to the challenge of three guys installing 16,000 square feet of turf. What was going on?

We didn't really have time to wallow in our pity so we just kept working. This job was definitely one of the most grueling projects I have ever done. The three of us worked from sun up to sun down for the next four days and even spent a little time working under the lights to get the job done. We were spreading nearly 50,000 pounds of crumb rubber by hand, shoveling out of a big bag into a wheelbarrow, carting the wheelbarrow to the dump spot, spreading it with the shovels again, moving it with the brooms, then power brooming it in.

Amazingly, we finished the job on the seventh day, Sunday. We had to because we were leaving from there to El Paso to set up for a home show that started on Monday. Finishing the fields was quite an accomplishment. We had completed the work in good time and had done a great job. We were once again able to fulfill a promise that we had made without truly knowing in the beginning just how we would complete it. Times like that make me feel especially good.

We rolled out of Deming on Sunday afternoon. We were really tired, but energized, and we made the two hour drive in our truck to El Paso. This was an exciting trip. Since arriving in Albuquerque about 16 months earlier, we had established a solid business, expanded our territory with AstroLawn to Tucson, and had expanded our footprint to central Florida with Ty. Now El Paso would be the start of our next new market. What better way to start into the market than participating in a home show?

This wasn't going to be the standard home show booth. The El Paso show was different from ones we had done before. First, it lasted an entire week. Second, they were constructing a model home in the middle of the exhibit hall. We were installing about 1,500 square feet of turf for the landscaping around the model home. We weren't paid to do this, but we did get the exposure. Our turf was the centerpiece of the show, and we had signage there in addition to our booth space.

This was a lot of turf and a lot of money. However, we knew we had to invest in our business to grow. Even though it was cut up for the install, we planned on bringing the turf we were installing around the model home back with us to Albuquerque and we would be able to resell most of it. The opportunity with all the leads we would generate (as we had learned from our Albuquerque shows) would quickly pay us back many times over.

We arrived in El Paso in the late afternoon. We went straight into the exhibit hall, unloaded the truck, and got to work installing turf. The show set up was supposed to close at 6:00 p.m. We really didn't pay attention to that. We knew we were there until it was done and that the show opened at 10:00 a.m. the next morning. The goal was set.

Brian, Rueben, and I worked all through the night. As we were installing the turf, my mind couldn't help but wander. Just one week ago, we were leaving Albuquerque for Deming to install the ball fields. To me it seemed like a lifetime ago. Over that week, we had spent over 90 hours working hard installing turf and another six hours driving. We hadn't spent much time sleeping or eating that was for sure. In my mind, I chuckled as I thought about Steve leaving after a day and then Randy and the Tucson crew going home. I thought about how we had 2,000-pound bags of rubber infill and no way to lift or move them. The sound of two power brooms' engines whining, almost making their own symphony for 12 hours a day the last two days, still echoed in my ears.

Could that have really all happened in just a week? My aching back, incredibly sore calf muscles and calloused hands confirmed for me that it had happened. Now we were staking our claim on El Paso. It was certainly different, but it did remind me of the cell phone purchase in Albuquerque. This home show was the start of a new territory for us. Once the people saw us at this show, we were committed. We weren't quite sure how we were going to service this market since we didn't have anyone ready to move. We just knew we would figure it out.

As the sun was coming up, we were finishing the installation of the turf around the model house. We then shot over to our booth, put down some turf, set up the backdrop, and we were off. Eli and Richard were coming down from Albuquerque for the show. That was a huge relief. As much as I would have liked to be there to work the show, we needed the break and we had much more to do in Albuquerque. We had some sales calls to run and a week's worth of office work to catch up on. Of course, we also wanted to see our families. Coming off trips like this, I would look forward to the welcome reception of my kids and Lorie. I loved to steal a few minutes to just play with the kids or sit on the couch and snuggle with them. Those are precious moments.

The drive back was long. The four-hour trip seemed to take forever, and staying awake was as difficult as the work we had done the previous week. The battle between the heavy eyelids and longing heart was won by the heart and we arrived safely back in Albuquerque. We dropped off Rueben, took the trailer to the warehouse, and then headed back home. While it would have been nice to get home and crawl into bed, I had four excited children and a beautiful wife who were ready to see their father/husband and I was ready to see them.

Brian

Sports are a passion for Karmies. We love the competition and even more, we love to win. I think that is one reason we enjoy business so much because it gives us the opportunity to compete and win.

Working with AstroLawn had put us in the position of being close to the big dog in the sports turf world, their sister company, AstroTurf. Yet we were still a little on the outside looking in. We tried several times to convince some of the AstroTurf team that we were capable of running field projects, but it wasn't an easy sell. Then one day, AstroTurf made that call to the bullpen.

In early February 2004, they called and we were given the opportunity to install four baseball infields in Deming, New Mexico. Finally, we had a breakthrough. It was a big installation and we were able to combine our love of sports and turf. The deal was, we'd get paid upon completion with no money up front. This meant that we had to come up with money for supplies like rubber infill, adhesive, and labor on our own. We were still on our winter slow-down in Albuquerque so we had the time, but that made it even harder on the money front. The good news was, we felt like we were starting to break through and this was going to be our year. This large install project would be a great kickoff to what was sure to be our best year yet.

We scrambled and scraped. We came up with all the cash we could muster, but still needed money to buy the rubber infill. At this point, we still had zero credit available, so we called our brother Ken and told him what was going on. Ken jumped right on it. With us only needing the advance for 30-60 days, and a strong company like AstroTurf being the payee—it seemed like a safe bet. Ken pulled some money from his investments and sent us a check. We were off and running.

Having recently cleared out our install crew, we started assembling a team to take on this project. Dale and I took two guys with us and met Randy and several guys from Tucson at the job site. Unfortunately, Deming had an unusual cold spell that week. Extreme low temperatures and even snow made the start of the project difficult. The weather conditions combined with long hard workdays resulted in much of our crew being scared off. After the first three days, we were left with Dale, me, and one worker from Albuquerque to finish our first sports field and the largest install we had ever tackled. It wasn't the glamorous project we had imagined, but it was quite a milestone for us.

I remember the sense of accomplishment looking at that finished project. We felt like we had just climbed a mountain and could enjoy the view. Maybe this was the start of many more sports fields, or maybe it was just the cash injection we needed to move our business forward. Either way, the possibilities were exhilarating.

We had finished up in Deming just in time to drive to El Paso and set up for a large home show there. We were excited to break into another new market and El Paso seemed like a great

Brian

fit. For the first time we wouldn't have to work the event; all we had to do was set up for the show. Eli and Richard were going to come cover the booth. We worked through the night installing turf at a couple locations in the expo center and headed back toward Albuquerque.

Now all that was left was to get the check and launch into our breakout year. Or so we thought.

Brian

CHAPTER TWENTY-TWO

The Call

Dale

I don't remember much about the Tuesday and Wednesday of that week in February, but Thursday is a day I will never forget.

We had a sales call that afternoon, and I told Brian I would run it. Sales calls for me were a love/hate relationship. I was really not much of a salesman at that time. I hadn't had much training in sales, and wasn't very comfortable "selling." It took me two years to get the courage to ask for the sale. Prior to that, customers had to initiate the close by telling me they wanted to go ahead and buy. Not exactly how you would teach it in a book.

The flip side of the coin was that I enjoyed meeting new people, talking with them, and helping them find solutions to their problems. I also enjoyed the sense of accomplishment when I would get a sale. It was like getting a win in a sporting event. Of course, I enjoyed the money, too.

Because of this, I would pull up to every house with a nervous excitement, and this one was no different. I don't remember the couple's name, although I wish I did, but I do remember that visit. They were an older couple and had a simple but nice home in the northeast part of Albuquerque. They met me at the door and invited me in. We exchanged greetings and I spent a few minutes talking about our products and our process. Things seemed to be going well and I suggested we go to the yard and look at the area where they wanted to have the turf installed.

I continued talking with them as I measured the area, but the ringing of my phone interrupted us. I glanced at the screen and saw it was Brian. I typically wouldn't answer my phone when with a customer, but since it was Brian, I excused myself and stepped away from the couple as I took the call.

"Hey, what's up?" I asked.

"Are you with the customer?" Brian asked.

"Yes, I am measuring the yard right now. Why?"

Brian's voice strained, "First, let me say that God is in control and sits on the throne. But … we are out of business. Wait, gotta go, I'll call you back."

With that, the call ended. What in the world was that? Did he just say we are out of business? Was this a joke? It sure didn't sound like one. I was somewhat stunned. What had happened? IRS? Some kind of accident?

I went back with the customers and finished measuring the area. As we were heading back into the house to give them the price, my phone rang again. It was Brian.

"Hello?"

"We are out of business. SRI Sports (the umbrella company over AstroLawn), just filed bankruptcy. Robert called to tell us AstroLawn is done and we are out of business. Whatever you do, don't take the check. Call me on your way home."

With that, Brian was gone again.

It felt like I staggered back into the house. I was confused. My gut ached. I felt numb. It was almost like an out of body experience. It was as though I watched myself bewildered, fighting to drag myself back into the house.

Once inside, I sat down on the couch. The couple asked me how much the turf would cost. I scratched out some calculations on the paper in front of me and came back with about $6,000.

"Great!" they said. "We want to go ahead and do it. How much do we need to put down?"

Brian's words rang in my ears, "We are out of business. Whatever you do, don't take a check."

I stammered, searching for words, "Well, uh … we require 50% down, but let me go back to the office and check the schedule first."

"That's ok. We can write you the check for the down payment. You can get back to us with the schedule."

We went back and forth a few times with them trying to give me a check to close the deal, and me trying not to sell it. In the end, I relented and took the check. I told them I would call them in the next day or two with an installation date. With that, I headed out the door.

Once in the car, my fingers started flying as I dialed up Brian on the cell phone.

"What's going on?" I asked him.

He proceeded to explain that he received a call from Robert at SRI Sports informing him that the cops were escorting people out of the building. The company had filed bankruptcy and everyone was being removed from their offices. They had told Brian that it was over, AstroLawn was no more, and we were out of business.

How could this be? We had chosen AstroLawn, in part, because of their size and prominence in the market place. How could we wake up one day and have them just be gone?

"Ok. I'm on my way back. Let me hang up and call Lorie. I'll see you in a few minutes."

"Oh, how'd the appointment go?" Brian asked.

"Good. They want us to do their yard. I took the check," I replied.

Were we not in such an embattled state at that moment, I am sure Brian would have given me some grief. As it were, what we were going to do with that check and how we would complete that job were not the major things we had to focus on at this moment.

I called Lorie. That was a tough call. As usual, she exceeded all expectations. She didn't quite understand what I was telling her, but she responded with, "I believe in you and that God has a purpose for us."

With that, I got off the phone, finished the short drive back to the office, and headed in to see Brian. While I had been on the sales call, Brian had the unenviable task of not only fielding these calls and trying to wrap his head around the news, but he also was the one who had to call Randy and Ty. Here were two guys, on opposite ends of the country that had both made a career and complete life change to join us in the AstroLawn business.

Brian

It's a moment I'll never forget. Some things just get burned into your mind. Sometimes it's great moments, sometimes it is bad moments, maybe it's just ordinary moments, but some things stay with you like the moment they happened. That call on the February afternoon is one of those moments.

We had been back from Deming for just a couple days, and I

was in the office while Dale was running a sales call. It was in the afternoon, and the phone rang. I picked it up to find Robert from the AstroLawn Corporate office (SRI Sports) on the other end. Normally Robert was calling to tell us we needed to pay on our turf orders, sometimes he'd just call to check in and see how we were doing. I expected this call might be a check up on how the Deming field installs went, and I was excited to tell him how well they turned out. But this time, Robert had a different tone.

"Brian, I only have a minute, but I wanted to call you guys first. It's over, we're out of business."

I chuckled, "Come on Robert, what's up really?"

"Seriously, it's over. We are out of business. All of SRI Sports including AstroTurf and AstroLawn are closing due to a forced bankruptcy. You are out of business. You need to shut down immediately, take down your signs, and stop doing business. There are armed guards escorting people out of the office here in Texas. It is over. I've got to go call some other dealers, but I wanted to call you and Dale first."

Then Robert was gone and I could feel my dreams starting to go with him. What about our upcoming breakout year? What about all the orders we had placed, but hadn't received yet? What about the money from the Deming field installs that we needed to pay back Ken's loan? What about all of the investment that we had made promoting AstroLawn? What now?

After I hung up the phone with Robert, I was reeling. What just happened? I realized I had to let Dale know and let him know quickly before he took a check from the sales call he was on.

I dialed Dale's number and he answered. I could tell he was in front of the customer so we couldn't talk much. I wasn't sure

Brian

what to say anyway. It just kind of came out.

"Robert called, something about armed guards and AstroLawn being shut down today. We are out of business. We'll figure it out when you get back here, just don't take a check. We don't have anything to sell."

I hung up. My words were probably as confusing and frustrating to Dale as Robert's were to me. I'm not even sure I knew what I was saying. Even worse, I realized that was just the first of several calls I needed to make. I needed to let Ty and Randy know quickly. They were going to hear it soon from Robert and I wanted them to hear it from me first.

Even worse, I had to call Angie. How was I going to tell my wife who had sacrificed so much over the past 16 months and who was now 7 months pregnant and 2,000 miles away from her family that our business was evaporating? I dialed the phone and listened to the ring. "Hello."

"Honey, are you sitting down?" I started.

"Why? What's up?" she half-laughed back.

"Seriously, please sit down." At this moment, especially with her pregnancy, I was actually fearful that she might faint.

When she assured me that she was seated, I went on to explain very briefly what was going on. I told her not to say anything to Lorie yet, but Dale and I would be calling both of them soon to talk through the situation. I tried to convince her that we'd get through this and all would be well. While I knew that to be true, I'm sure my tone was far from confident. Angie was a gem. While she was obviously shaken, she reassured me that she trusted we were in this place for a reason and that she knew we'd figure it out. Now, on to Ty.

Brian

The Call

Orlando is a few hours ahead of Albuquerque, so when I reached Ty, I was interrupting his dinner. In fact, it was a dinner with his in-laws who had just moved from Ohio to Florida to join his AstroLawn team.

I don't remember the exact words I used but I know Ty could tell something was serious from my tone. He excused himself from the table and we talked for a couple of minutes about what had just happened. I let him go so he could share the news with his family and we agreed to catch back up when Dale returned.

The call with Randy was similar. Stunned silence was the response.

I was numb. These calls hurt. The responsibility I felt for each of these families being in this situation was like a giant lead weight resting on my shoulders. I had moved my family across the country and Dale had done the same. On top of that, we had enlisted others to join this audacious adventure. Randy and his family moved from Arkansas to Arizona. Ty moved his family from Indiana to Florida and passed up a great job opportunity in Denver. Ty's in-laws had moved from Ohio to Florida. Five families all involved in cross-country moves and life altering career changes fueled by our crazy notion to chase greener grass with artificial turf just 18 months prior. What were we thinking? Had we just jumped off a cliff and taken others with us. I felt like we were free falling without a parachute.

This was a defining moment for many reasons. The dominos that led to this point and our response to the situation would forever change our lives. The emotions we felt would leave a lasting impression as well. Actions have consequences. Right or wrong, we had influenced others with our actions and now felt the responsibility of not just our families, but also the others we had brought with us. This lesson has served us well as we've

Brian

175

built our ForeverLawn team. We feel this responsibility and we take it seriously just as much or even more today. Sometimes we feel it too much and we have to remind ourselves that God is in control, not us. We can't let this weight paralyze us, but it is a responsibility as well as an honor.

These lessons would come over time, but right now just one question was ringing in my head—what next?

CHAPTER TWENTY-THREE

The Next Chapter

Dale

Deep breath in. Deep breath out. What would we do now? As I arrived back at the office, Brian and I decided the first thing we would do is get all three of us on the phone to talk through our situation. Ty was not only a partner in business; he was also our best friend and someone whose opinion we greatly respected.

On the call, the first thing we did was to pray. We asked God for wisdom and discernment, for the ability to sift through all the information, challenges, and emotions, and for the ability to determine what we should do. We then made a short list of our options.

First, we could pack it all in and go back to Ohio. We had no roots in New Mexico, nothing to really anchor us there. This seemed logical. Second, we could try to find another turf company to be associated with, but we were AstroLawn. All of our marketing material, advertising, and promotion was building that brand for us. Third, we could stay in New Mexico and just leave the grass idea behind and move on to something else.

We had quit our jobs, left our homes, and moved our families to start this business in New Mexico. As we looked at it, we had already really lost everything. We figured that if we were already all in, we had nothing left to lose. We might as well move forward and see what would happen. I believe God answered our prayers for wisdom and discernment, and we pretty quickly agreed that we would just continue to move forward in the turf business. We had no idea how or with whom, but nonetheless, we were pressing on.

Brian

Dale got back to the office and we started to regroup. Robert had sent an email copying all of the AstroLawn dealers and we read it together. We talked to Angie and Lorie and let them know what was going on. We spent that night talking, thinking, and praying. We got on the phone with Ty and talked through the options.

Through this process, we realized something. We weren't out of business, our supplier was. We weren't forced into bankruptcy, that was SRI Sports. We didn't have any armed guards escorting us out or closing our office. In fact, everything in our office was in good shape. Heck, against my request, Dale had just made a sale and taken the check.

Maybe this wasn't the end. There are other suppliers, right? I mean, we can sell this stuff, and we are seeing good traction in three different markets. Synthetic grass works, and its use as a landscape option is only going to grow. We just need a new product to represent.

As Dale, Ty, and I spent the night thinking and talking through this, we decided to start making a list of what we were looking for in a supplier. First, we wanted someone we could trust. Too many companies in this industry seemed to lack integrity. We often said that we'd rather fail in business with our integrity in tact than make money at the expense of our integrity. What would it profit us to gain the whole world and lose our soul? We had to have high integrity from the company we represented.

Second, we wanted the best product out there. We didn't want to sell anything with inferior quality. We had to be able to pass our own grocery store test. We wanted to be able to hold our head up high and ask how they liked their yard whenever we did see customers in public.

Finally, we wanted the ability to develop and sell products that went beyond just landscapes. We had pushed AstroLawn on the idea of new products and even a product designed for playgrounds, but they had balked at the idea.

From what we had seen, these were the items missing in the turf industry; integrity, quality, and innovation. If we could find a way to fill this void, we felt the best was yet to come.

There was definitely hope but there was also reality. That night and the next few weeks left us emotionally and mentally drained as we swung on the pendulum of possibilities. On one end was the potential for success and even new opportunities, on the other was the possibility that our venture was ending. The floor had fallen out beneath us, but perhaps the ceiling had been lifted as well. While we saw opportunity, we also felt the pull of the present reality.

Coming out of the winter, we didn't have any cash reserves, and with customers we couldn't supply and projects we couldn't complete, the cash flow picture looked to be getting bleaker. On top of that, the AstroLawn brand name that we had spent tens of thousands of dollars and 18 months promoting in Albuquerque was gone. The bankruptcy of our supplier would fuel rumors and deceit that our competition could (and would) use against us. Perhaps worst of all, the $40,000 we were owed for the sports field project we completed in Deming was wiped out in bankruptcy.

It was a long night of talking, praying, and thinking. It was one of the longest nights of our lives.

179

CHAPTER TWENTY-FOUR

Value Added

Dale

Brian and I got into the office early on Friday morning. We were greeted by an interesting and pleasant surprise. We had a voice mail from someone at an artificial turf company. They had heard about what happened with AstroLawn and were wondering if we would be interested in offering their products.

This was great. Maybe we wouldn't have to go find a solution. Maybe the solution was going to find us. We called the company back and began discussing possible options. Then we received another call. This one was from a sports field company that was interested in expanding in the landscape market. They wanted to talk to us about becoming a dealer for them. Wow. In just a few short hours, we went from not knowing how we would proceed, to having a choice between two possibilities.

At that moment, it was as if a light bulb went off. We had value. We were in the industry, had established a good footprint in Albuquerque, and we presented opportunity for other companies. We began to think about the other AstroLawn dealers. There must have been about twenty of them by now. If we had power as one entity, the group of us should have much more. Could we leverage this group buying power into a good deal for all of us?

The phones were busy that day. We were calling dealers, talking with suppliers, calling Ty, calling Randy and on it went. It was actually somewhat exciting. Where would all of this take us?

We also had Eli and Richard to deal with. Word travels fast, so it wasn't completely surprising that we got a call from Eli asking what was going on. Competitors at the El Paso show had come up to them and told them AstroLawn was out of business. They were telling customers that too. We explained to Eli what was going on and reassured him we were not out of business. Our supplier may be gone, but we were working on getting that corrected. We just told him to finish the show the same way they had started. We weren't going anywhere.

Through that day and over the weekend, we were evaluating who we were, what our purpose was, and how we would go about achieving it. We had been given a clean slate. We needed to plot a new course, and then go after it.

Brian

The next morning, the sun came up just like it had the day before. I'm pretty sure I saw it happen, because I don't think I slept. Amazing how a sunrise can bring the feeling of newness and remind me that this creation is much bigger than our pinpoint view. While that helped give some perspective, our heads were spinning.

We decided to do what we had always done and we headed into the office. We had a few jobs pending that we'd need to complete, and all we could do at this point was take it one-step at a time, controlling what we could and walking in faith in what we couldn't see.

We went back to the e-mail announcing the SRI shutdown and realized it had all the email addresses for the other dealers on it. At the AstroLawn conference eight months ago, we had established a rapport with many of these dealers and had since talked to several of them giving some advice on where we were finding success. We decided to send an email to all of these dealers realizing they were in the same position as us. Maybe if all of us pulled together, we could use our collective buying power to represent another turf company. Maybe this could work. We scheduled a conference call with these AstroLawn dealers and began to formulate a plan.

As we got on the conference call, we realized that while there was value to this plan, we were trying to herd cats. There were over twenty different AstroLawn dealers with as many different ideas. Some saw the turf industry as a full time venture, others had just been kicking the tires of this thing or were adding it to what they already did.

As we talked, there were two emerging visions for how to move forward. We led one vision focused on taking our time to find the right supplier and thinking long term with integrity, quality, and new products as our standard. These were the values we saw missing in the turf industry and just the way we wanted to conduct business. The other vision was focused more on moving quickly. Striking while the iron was hot and finding the cheapest product available to make money as soon as possible and then get out of the turf industry. This viewpoint stunned us. This was completely opposite of anything we wanted to be associated with and didn't fit our long-term vision.

Over the next few weeks, we had several phone calls, email exchanges, and discussions. The gap between our visions widened and our alliance weakened. A slight few shared our vision; Ty, Bill from Boise, Idaho, a couple other dealers from New Mexico, and a dealer from Orange County, California. Either the rest of the AstroLawn dealer contingent hung up their turf shoes, or they joined the cheap and fast crowd. It was disappointing that we didn't have more, but we felt confident in our decision.

I've heard it said that, "people of integrity expect to be believed, and when they're not, they let time prove them right." I

Brian

guess in the end, this statement played out here. To our knowledge, none of those who chose the cheap and fast route are still in the industry today, nor made the money they hoped. Those of us that chose the narrow path have been blessed to be a part of a business with tens of thousands of satisfied customers and millions of square feet of grass sold over the past ten years. We were just warming up.

Things didn't happen in a flash and ForeverLawn certainly wasn't born in a day. In fact, at the point we split from the cheap and fast crowd, we still weren't sure where we were heading, we just had an idea of what it would look like. The name ForeverLawn and the idea of owning our own national turf company hadn't crossed our minds yet. All we knew is that we wanted to find a business with integrity, quality, and innovation that we could be proud to represent.

Brian

CHAPTER TWENTY-FIVE

One Direction

Dale

While we were trying to determine the path our organization would take next, back in El Paso the show had finished up. We told Eli and Richard to make sure to bring the grass back from the show. We had the 1,500 square feet of turf we had installed around the model home. That grass had become even more important because without a supplier, we had no more grass. We would have to get by in the immediate with any standing inventory we had.

In spite of this request, they returned to Albuquerque empty handed. When we asked where the turf was, they said it was too hard to load so they left it there. That was a lot of money and opportunity that was thrown away, right at a time when we would need it most.

That next week was a combination of trying to fulfill commitments we had made to customers (like the check I took) and working to find our new direction. We talked with Priscilla, Eli, and Richard on Monday, explaining what all had happened and where we stood on things.

This would prove to be a pivotal point in what we would become. We made the decision for quality over commodity. We chose to create something with lasting value, not something just to make fast-money. We chose to put a stake in the ground, claim this as what we would do and who we would become, and we chose to center it on integrity. We were looking for something bigger than just the artificial turf. We were looking for grass without limits.

After several days of gathering data on what was available, we had a list of about 20 possibilities. We began to trim the list down; not just based on the products, but also the companies and the people that represented them. By the end of week two, we realized that what we wanted in the market place was pretty scarce. There were companies we liked, but they didn't have the right product. We found products we liked, but the companies didn't promote or share our values. Our list of possible options was narrowed down to about two or three.

Meanwhile, in our office our sales people were getting restless. It had now been over two weeks since AstroLawn had closed its doors, and we still had no product and no direction. We had a home show in Albuquerque, and Brian and I chose not to work the show. We asked Eli and Richard to run it. This would free up our time to continue looking for the right solution. I know it was a tough task for the guys, since we didn't have any real products to show. We told them to just show what we had and promote the idea of artificial grass. We were still working on selling some inventory and as soon as we had a new direction, we would discuss it with the potential customer on the actual sales call.

Coming out of the home show, Eli brought us some samples of turf someone showed him at the show. He wanted us to buy it and sell that product. While it looked great as a sample, we weren't convinced it offered the quality answer we were looking for. This led to a heated argument between Eli and me. He was upset we weren't listening to him; and I was frustrated that he didn't understand our vision and the need for both a quality product and a trustworthy company.

It wasn't more than a few days after the meeting that Eli came into the office and announced he was done. He said he couldn't sell for us any more if we just summarily dismissed his ideas. With that, he walked out, and he took Richard with him.

In pretty short order, we realized that this move was going to hurt a lot more than just losing our main salesman. No, this was a move that would easily cost us a couple hundred thousand dollars. Not only did Eli leave, but he also took all of the leads from the El Paso show,

and much closer to home, he took all of the leads from the Albuquerque Home Show with him. These shows were our lifeblood, and
should have generated $150,000 or more in revenue. In all the chaos
and emotion of AstroLawn being gone, looking for a new supplier
and product, and trying to keep our heads above water, we had never
received the lead list from either of the shows. Just like that, it was all
gone.

Apparently, we were taking the fast lane from bad to worse because
within a week, we learned that Richard and Eli had opened up a new
artificial turf shop right down the street from our office. They had
become dealers for another artificial turf supplier. Needless to say,
their business got off to a great start with about 200 quality leads in
both the Albuquerque and El Paso markets. That one stung a little, to
say the least.

Sifting through pages of notes and boxes of samples, we identified a
product that really intrigued us. It was different than the rest in that
it had a multi-layered quality backing. It used blades that were more
durable and longer lasting. The blades also had some texture, and
although they weren't as soft and appealing as some of the new blade
structures, the quality of the product was evident.

In our talks with this company, we found the closest place we could
see an installation was in Southern California. By this time, we had
been "out of business" for about three weeks. We knew we needed
to see this product. We couldn't leave the direction of our company
to chance.

Brian, Derek (my 11-year old son), and I loaded up in the car and
headed for California. It was about a 13-hour trip. We didn't have
money for a hotel, so we left in the evening and drove all through
the night. We were going to meet the west coast sales representative,
Greg, in the morning in Los Angeles and he would then show us
around to see some field installations with this product.

One Direction

No doubt, the excitement of charting the path that lay ahead helped us make the long drive to California. We rolled into Denny's in L.A at about 10:00 a.m., and Greg was waiting for us there. We made our introductions, got something to eat, and then hopped in Greg's car for the whirlwind tour. Greg was a gracious host, and he showed us several field installs that looked great. What we saw that day convinced us we had found the right product. After a long day of driving around Los Angeles, it was time to head back home.

As we experienced many times before, the late night drive back home was difficult. The Mojave Desert seemed to go on forever. God was good to us. As I hit a very tired point where my eyes were becoming more closed than open, a light rain fell from the desert sky. I put my head out the window and the cool rain hitting my face woke me up enough to keep going. We ended up back in Albuquerque early the next morning, excited that maybe we had found our new product. Now we had to work out the details.

Brian

We took our spreadsheet of potential suppliers and turf companies and started whittling it down based on this integrity, quality, and innovation criteria. Some were crossed off due to integrity issues, some due to less than ideal quality, and some couldn't get past just asking us to sell the standard product that they already made. We just weren't finding anyone with the complete package.

We did find one unique company out there who seemed to have a good bit of what we wanted. It wasn't perfect, but it might be a fit. It was a sports field company. They had a product that was different than anything we had seen. It had a very durable blade structure, included a couple different kinds of grass blades, and they were even experimenting with a new type of backing. We felt this one may just have potential.

After we had several conversations with the three partners, and a road trip to California to visit some of their installs, we decided we might be able to make this work. We put some basic ideas together and asked them to start a landscape division. To our dismay, they felt their focus needed to stay on sports fields. In return, they suggested that we start a landscape turf company and they would supply us the turf. They apparently didn't know what our bank account looked like. We didn't have the money to fund a startup and we surely weren't in a position to get a loan.

After a little more thought, we came back with what we thought was an even better idea. They should hire the three of us to start the landscape division for them. Here is the answer! They have a product, but didn't have the understanding of the landscape market or a way to get it to the marketplace. We have the knowledge of this side of the industry and the ability to introduce the product into six or seven local markets instantly. Plus a paycheck for us sounded really sweet. It had been a long time since we had a steady pay. That would give us the stability we needed because we were certainly in need of some solid financial footing.

Again, their answer was no. They had no desire to hire us and really didn't want to invest into this new landscape market. They could sell us the product, but that was it. We were on our own to come up with a landscape and recreation focused turf company.

Dale, Ty, and I continued to think through this. We had to find a turf supply for our local markets, and if we wanted any chance at working with those few ex-AstroLawn dealers that shared our vision, we had to make something happen. It was well into the spring now and we were losing the good selling season.

Brian

One Direction

Was there a way to make this work? What if we did create a company to supply ourselves? We didn't have money, but maybe it wouldn't take much. Maybe this was the direction we were supposed to go.

CHAPTER TWENTY-SIX

Blessings in Disguise

Dale

For all the good things we had done, and all the challenges we had overcome, we almost got tripped up by our own little thinking. The company that had the product we wanted was a small field company. They didn't have a brand and really had nothing for us beyond a product. We were AstroLawn dealers previously, and now our thinking was to be dealers for another company.

This is one of those times when God presented us with an opportunity, the closing of AstroLawn, and we didn't take it. We were standing at an open door but not walking through it. God pushed the issue and showed us another opportunity with this new product. This time, he made it more obvious with the company encouraging us not to just be dealers but to start our own business. We pushed back.

Ultimately, we stepped through the opportunity God provided, but He really had to guide us. The company simply wouldn't make us dealers. If we wanted to sell this product, we would have to create a new entity. Our hesitation really rose from the fact that we had no money and little knowledge with which to start. We focused more on the reasons we couldn't than the reasons we could do this. However, we did finally make the move, put our plans in place, and began the next leg in our journey.

Once we were over the hurdle of committing to start the new business, we started to get pretty excited. We knew what our product was going to be, but we needed a name, and we needed to create an image that portrayed what we were trying to create.

We had meetings and phone calls with Ty to try to find a name. We began making a list. We just shot names back and forth, and discussed them. What did they mean? What did they convey? We had just gone through this entire process of determining how we would move forward in the turf business because we wanted something that would be long term, something we could be proud of ten, twenty, maybe even thirty years later. We wanted something that we could associate with our family name, and we wanted something that our kids could do with us when they grew up. We all liked the name ForeverLawn.

Brian

To add more excitement to this timeframe, on Easter Sunday 2004, our third daughter, Meredith Grace, was born. It was a difficult birth and I remember seeing concern in the eyes of the doctor and nurses as they immediately took our baby to a nearby table and began working on little Meredith. I could tell our baby was struggling to breathe and she was turning colors. I stayed with Angie and tried to ensure her that everything was good while keeping one eye on our fragile newborn. After just a few minutes, a perfectly healthy baby girl was given to her mother, but for those few moments in between, that uncertainty hung heavy.

Sometimes birth isn't easy and sometimes it doesn't go as planned. However, moments of uncertainty aren't necessarily bad. Sometimes they are just part of the process we have to go through to get where we want to go.

After six weeks of muddling through our turf wilderness, we decided that creating this new company was the direction we were supposed to take. Like we had many times before, we decided to just take action. We didn't know how it would all work, but we could see far enough ahead to take the next step, and that was all we needed. We chose to roll the dice one more time and just do what we could. The cost seemed reasonable to incorporate, so in addition to being my 28th birthday, April 22, 2004 was the official birth of ForeverLawn, Inc.

We figured that we could use office facilities and equipment we already had going for our existing businesses, so we did. ForeverLawn was started with a very meager beginning. No fanfare, no outside funding, and really no expectations. It was formed with a desire to answer the question of who would be the supplier that we were proud to represent.

We knew what we wanted in the Albuquerque and Orlando local markets. We wanted to represent a national company built on integrity, quality, and innovation. We wanted to be a part of something bigger than just ourselves. We knew we could get a product from anywhere, but if there wasn't a bigger presence behind our local market, it just wouldn't grow into what it could be.

God used the SRI bankruptcy to move us through a new open door, one that we never would have gone through on our own. Without any cash to invest, or a loan to draw from, we started ForeverLawn. We became what we felt was missing in the industry. We funded it by selling jobs in our local markets and selling the turf to our affiliated dealers at a small mark up. Every time we had an extra dollar, we invested it back into our business. We realized now more than ever, we needed to practice delayed gratification.

Without knowing what we were really doing, we had painted a mental picture of what this national turf business should be and we started building toward that vision day by day.

Brian

Dale

Experience is a great teacher. We had come out of one of the most tumultuous times of our lives in a much better place. We were not out of business. In fact, we were far from it. We had not only survived the closing of AstroLawn and the end of that business, we had used that event to launch a completely new direction. We now had two entities that were separate but part of the same vision. Ty also created a new entity for his local business in Florida. With that, ForeverLawn officially had its first two dealers. We were no longer just the local representation in the Albuquerque market, we were a brand. We could define where we went from here. How much reach we would have, what our products were like, and what markets we chose to compete in was now all in our hands.

In the spring of 2004, ForeverLawn was officially launched. This company would soon become a recognized brand in the industry, and over time would establish its place as the leader in quality, integrity, and innovation in the artificial grass industry. God had blessed us with a new direction and a fresh start. He had moved us to a place we couldn't have arrived at on our own. In hindsight, everything that had happened played out for a purpose and created the perfect launching point for our new venture. I marvel in amazement at how God does that.

Brian

As we stretched and saved to find money to invest into ForeverLawn, we realized we needed an identity. It only made sense that a website was a great place to start, but how would we make it and what would even go on it? We wanted a consistent image, something easily recognizable and professional, but we had no idea how or what. We started to develop a website on our own through PowerPoint, but it looked more like a junior high project than a business.

Being a fledgling business running out of a small strip plaza in Albuquerque, we took advantage of our surroundings. Our printer was either not working or non-existent so we started borrowing printing capability from our next-door neighbors, Bocotek, a printer and IT company. One day, when going next door to pick up some printed papers from their office, I noticed a new face in the front room. Being a start-up themselves (and probably trying to recoup some of our printing costs), Bocotek had leased space to a friend of theirs, Donna Kent, who had a marketing business. I introduced myself to Donna and then proceeded to the back room to pick up my prints. On the way down the small hallway, I noticed some framed images of different company logos. The businesses didn't seem to have any connection to each other but all had neat looking logos. That was it; we needed one of these too. I poked my head back into Donna's office and asked what all these framed logo images were from.

"I designed those," she said. "That's what I do, brand development and marketing."

I wasn't even sure what brand development was but I liked those logos. They looked sharp and professional. They gave me a good feeling about the companies they represented. They were memorable and made me want to know more.

"I think we might need a logo," I replied. "Do you make websites too?"

So began a relationship that would again change the trajectory of ForeverLawn. We took the little money we had and engaged Donna Kent of DK Marketing to develop a logo and a website for us. We gave Donna the basic content we wanted on the site and some very basic directives; make it clean and professional.

Donna did just that and more. With her help, we developed

Brian

the ForeverLawn logo that we've used for over ten years, and shortly after that, we launched a new website promoting our new national turf brand. Then we created some local marketing material that spun off this national image. Things were starting to click. Now we weren't just a couple guys in Albuquerque or Orlando peddling turf; now we had the credibility of a national brand behind us. We (at least in appearance) were a part of something bigger.

As we continued to invest in marketing and advertising, more business came in and we dumped all of our new profit right back into more marketing. We weren't dumb, stick with the hot hand. Donna was doing a great job taking our vision for what we wanted to be and putting it into images and words.

Having been AstroLawn dealers for a year and a half, but never having the marketing tools we wanted, we used this opportunity to develop the marketing materials we needed to create a professional and trustworthy image in our local markets. This ground up innovation led to marketing designed with the local dealer in mind. We created brochures, folders, flyers, and more that presented the image of a quality product and a strong national brand. Then we tailored them to our local markets. It worked and our dealerships continued to grow.

It didn't take long, and people started responding to our advertising and finding this impressive new website of ours. We had potential customers from all over the country contacting us. In addition, we had another type of inquiry we were responding to: potential dealers.

As we worked to design this new ForeverLawn website, we decided to create a page offering dealership opportunities. We didn't know exactly what this would look like, but we always had the thought of helping other entrepreneurs start their own businesses. When we were with AstroLawn, we had developed

Brian

195

a little bit of a mentor relationship with some of the other dealers and felt it would be great to continue helping new businesses. Besides, why reinvent the wheel? We had gone through many struggles and learned through much trial and error. Why not help these new businesses learn from our mistakes and our successes. On top of that, we realized the benefit of having a strong brand behind the local dealership. How much faster could we have gotten started if we would have had training, marketing material, and product support? We knew the power of sharing this opportunity and we put the offer out there.

One after another, we had people from all over that wanted to buy these ForeverLawn products and some even wanted to represent them in their local markets. Dale and I spent our days operating and working our local Albuquerque dealership and then spent all night on our computers operating and developing ForeverLawn, Inc. We spent much time helping new dealers develop ForeverLawn businesses and we spent many hours responding to customer inquiries and answering emails.

ForeverLawn was taking more time and money than it was generating, but we could feel the momentum and knew something bigger than us was happening. While our local dealership grew and became profitable, we continued to take those profits and put them into building ForeverLawn. Our course had been set, and now was not the time to look for comfort or to look around and check our progress, now was the time to keep our heads down and work.

Brian

CHAPTER TWENTY-SEVEN

The End of the Beginning

Dale

This was merely the beginning. It was the beginning of a venture that would create opportunity for hundreds of people to provide for themselves and others. The next 10 years would present new twists and turns that we could never have anticipated. If we had, we may never have launched on the journey. What lay ahead were some of the hardest times, so hard that it made the period from 2002 through the spring of 2004 seem easy. But it all had a purpose. As Paul so eloquently states in his letter to the Romans:

"And not only this, but we also exult in our tribulations, knowing that tribulation brings about perseverance; and perseverance, proven character; and proven character, hope; and hope does not disappoint, because the love of God has been poured out within our hearts through the Holy Spirit who was given to us."

The lessons we learned through these trials and successes are vast. Somehow, in order to win, we often have to lose. Even if things aren't all figured out, sometimes we just need to throw ourselves at something because action can trump fear. With family, faith, and maybe just the will power to follow up on an email, your belief in the journey that lies before you will be Forever strong.

Brian

The next 24 months would turn out to be even more of a roller coaster than our first 18. We would battle tremendous product issues, financial challenges, and business hurdles that made our start look like it was smooth sailing. However, our first 18 months were foundational for us. We learned what it was like to start a brand new business in a brand new market. We learned the challenges and successes of artificial turf and what it took to introduce this concept to customers and educate them on the benefits of this new synthetic grass. We learned what it was like to be a dealer of a national product. In short, we learned what we needed to build ForeverLawn.

In addition to the genesis of ForeverLawn, the spring of 2004 brought us a few team members that would play a large role in the growth of our business. While many of our sales team dissipated as we went through the transition from AstroLawn to ForeverLawn, one new salesman was just getting started. Joe Leedie joined our team in a sales role and filled a much-needed void. Over the next few years, Joe would wear multiple hats from sales and bookkeeping, to production and inventory management. One title he will always hold is being the first official ForeverLawn employee—even before Dale or me.

As we looked to rebuild our installation crew, a friend recommended their teenage brother who was coming to Albuquerque from Wisconsin—enter Josh Guelker. Josh started on installs and caught on quickly. His character and trustworthiness were a welcome change to the crew we had recently dismissed. As ForeverLawn grew, Josh grew with us taking on several different roles through the years.

Interesting how the pieces of our puzzle came to us at just the right time. I'd love to take the credit for seeking out the right people, but often it is just being open to the right person as they cross our paths. As we've grown, one key value we've held when adding team members is that we look for character fits first. Skill sets can be taught much more easily than character.

Our families' resolve and support continued throughout our journey. Today both of our brothers, Jim and Ken, work with us at ForeverLawn, but even before they were officially part of

Brian

this business, they contributed to the bigger picture of what we were accomplishing.

We continued to build ForeverLawn with the pursuit of integrity, quality, and innovation. Late in 2004, that drive for innovation served Ty well as the market in Florida wouldn't survive in landscape alone. Ty developed Playground Grass that provided a fall safe turf system that could be installed under play equipment instead of sand, wood fibers, or rubber surfacing. This surface met the fall safety standards under play equipment and provided wheelchair accessibility with all the look and feel of natural grass. The development of Playground Grass allowed the turf to not only be used around playgrounds, but under play equipment as well. This innovation changed the trajectory of ForeverLawn, and it greatly impacted the turf industry as a whole.

By early 2005, ForeverLawn had grown to about a dozen local dealerships across the U.S. and had built on our platform of integrity, quality, and innovation. Initially our innovation wasn't rocket science, but rather just responding to the opportunities visible in the marketplace. We were a different kind of turf company with owners and directors on the front lines. We saw the problems first hand and helped develop solutions that led the way for many to follow.

K9Grass was another ForeverLawn original based on a response to the marketplace. Within a year of launching ForeverLawn, we realized almost half of our inquiries mentioned a dog. While this was often used as a reason people didn't believe they could use artificial turf, we saw this as an opportunity to develop a solution. We changed the design of the turf to make it drain instantly, provide more durability, and even added an antimicrobial agent to the K9Grass blades to provide a cleaner safer environment.

Brian

The innovation list goes on and includes several patented and trademarked ideas, but the accomplishment we are most proud of has been in the way ForeverLawn operates, both with our internal team and with the business model we pursued. We had been in Corporate America and knew we never wanted to go back. What we wanted, and what we wanted to help others find, was freedom. We didn't want to develop a team of mind-numbed people chasing mundane tasks. We want to provide others the freedom to use their God-given talents to the best of their ability. Provide a framework for success, but not squeeze everyone into an identical mold.

We try to apply this formula throughout our business and to our dealer business model. Just as we did when we first expand-ed to Tucson and Orlando, we choose to bet on entrepreneurs when opening new markets. We have been blessed to work with some of the best and brightest in these ForeverLawn business-es and love seeing new dealers catch the vision and taste suc-cess. It is a gratifying experience and has become our favorite part of the business. This model has not just been successful financially; it has enriched our lives personally with friendships that go way beyond business. We have truly been blessed.

ForeverLawn is just scratching the surface of the opportuni-ty available for quality synthetic grass products and solutions. While we certainly don't know what the future holds, God willing, we will continue building this business on a constant pursuit of our core values of integrity, quality, and innovation. We are, and will continue to be, grass without limits.

Brian

CONCLUSION

In the editing process of this book, we had several requests for the conclusion of this story. Truthfully, there is no conclusion—the journey is just beginning and the number of stories between the ending of this book and today is a much longer volume than we've already written. It would be nearly impossible to record all of the people, events, and experiences that have shaped the past decade. However, it does seem appropriate to give readers a snapshot of where ForeverLawn is as of the publishing of this book.

ForeverLawn has never been Dale and Brian. Hopefully if you've read this far, that has been evident. From the beginning, we always felt this was bigger than us and we just feel blessed to be a part of it. The ForeverLawn team has grown from the humble beginnings we've written about here to a thriving international business.

Today, in 2015, the ForeverLawn team has grown to over 50 successful independent dealers in North America with sales on five different continents. We have more than 40 home office team members supporting these dealerships and growing the ForeverLawn brand.

Perhaps most exciting, we have had the honor of servicing over 10,000 customers and in the process we have sold over 15 million square feet of ForeverLawn turf. Our list of successful projects ranges from backyards to full scale sports facilities and from amusement parks to veterinarian hospitals. We've been privileged to install ForeverLawn on rooftops in major cities and on playing fields in desolate deserts. Every project is unique, but every one improving the lives of our customers—often in unexpected ways.

All of this is a great beginning for the story yet to be written. Can't wait to see what God has in store.

DuPont™ ForeverLawn®
Select Synthetic Grass

DuPont™ ForeverLawn® Select Synthetic Grass is the perfect solution for your landscape. Whatever your landscape need, DuPont™ ForeverLawn® Select Synthetic Grass provides a waterless, low-maintenance solution for years to come.

BEAUTIFUL • REALISTIC • CAREFREE
Find out more at: foreverlawn.com/dupont

K9Grass®

K9Grass provides an ideal surface for pets in both commercial and residential environments. K9Grass is the artificial grass designed specifically for dogs!

SAFE • DRAINABLE • CLEANABLE • DURABLE
Find out more at: k9grass.com

SplashGrass by ForeverLawn is a beautiful, safe, drainable synthetic grass that offers unique benefits for water play areas and landscaping within water parks.

Fun and functional from the first splash!
Find out more at: foreverlawn.com/splashgrass

SPORTSGRASS®

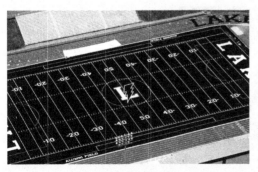

The leading-edge technology in SportsGrass is a great fit for your field or facility. The unique construction of our product creates a superior playing surface for both indoor and outdoor fields.

Playing at a higher level. Ultimate performance - natural feel.
Find out more at: sportsgrassturf.com

Made in the USA
Columbia, SC
24 September 2020